THE COUNTRY HOUSES OF SIR JOHN VANBRUGH

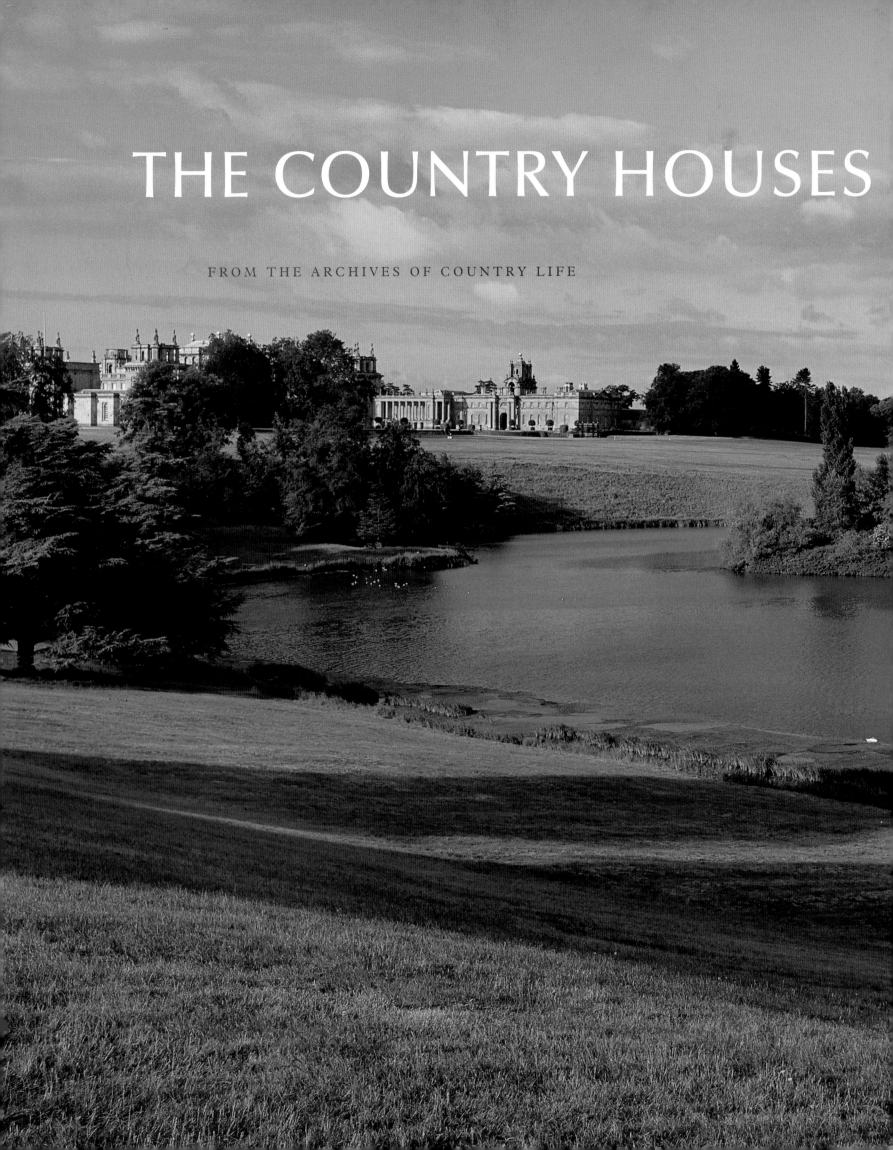

THE COUNTRY HOUSES

FROM THE ARCHIVES OF COUNTRY LIFE

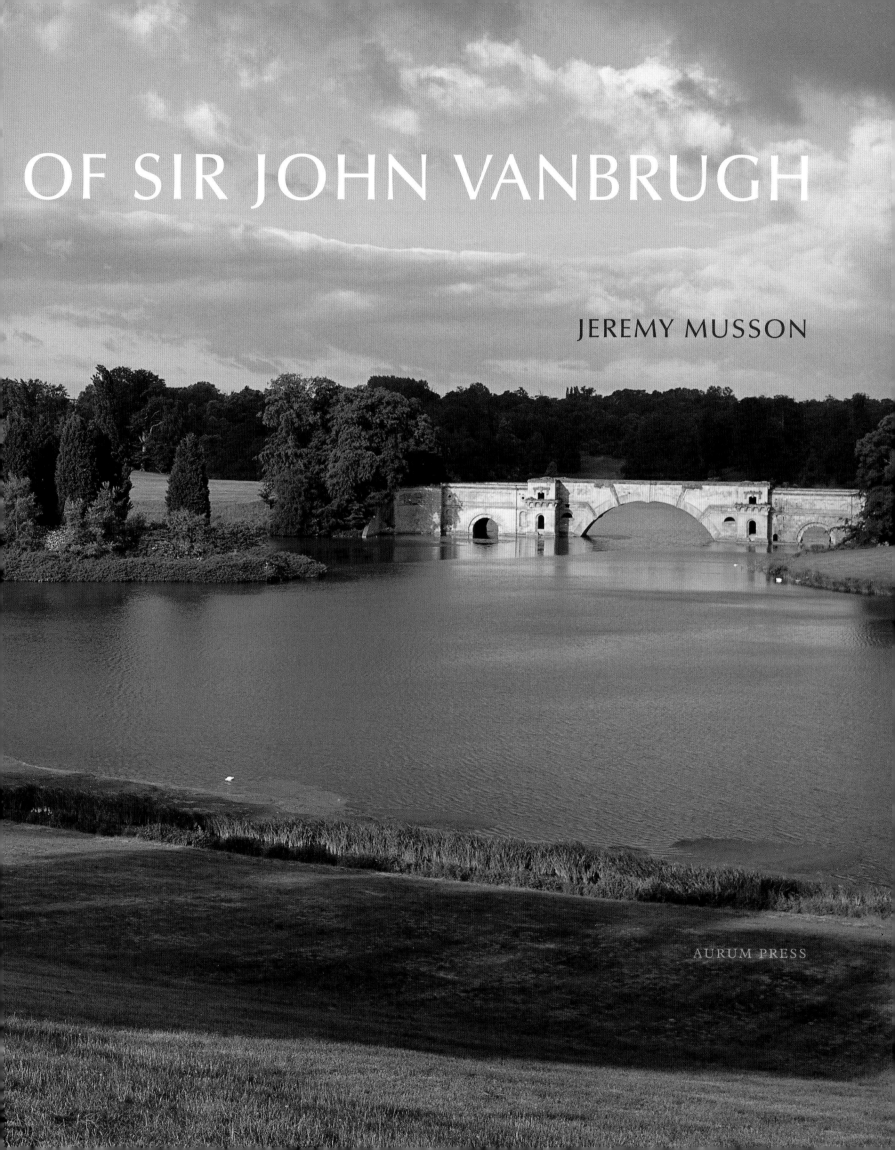

OF SIR JOHN VANBRUGH

JEREMY MUSSON

AURUM PRESS

This book is dedicated to my father, Roger,
for all his thoughtfulness, support and interest –
a very English gentleman

First published in Great Britain 2008 by Aurum Press Limited
7 Greenland Street, London NW1 0ND
www.aurumpress.co.uk

Text copyright © 2008 Jeremy Musson
Photographs © *Country Life* Picture Library

ISBN 978 1 84513 097 8
10 9 8 7 6 5 4 3 2 1
2012 2011 2010 2009 2008

Design by James Campus
Printed and bound in Singapore

Frontispiece: *Blenheim Palace, Oxfordshire.*
Front endpaper: *Castle Howard, Yorkshire. A detail of the gallery, which overlooks the Great Hall.*
Rear endpaper: *Blenheim Palace: A detail of the roof-line.*

THE COUNTRY LIFE PICTURE LIBRARY

The *Country Life* Picture Library holds a complete set of prints made from its negatives, and a card index to the subjects, usually recording the name of the photographer and the date of the photographs catalogued, together with a separate index of photographers. It also holds a complete set of *Country Life* and various forms of published indices to the magazine. The Library may be visited by appointment, and prints of any negatives it holds can be supplied by post.

For further information, please contact the Library Manager, Justin Hobson, at *Country Life*, Blue Fin Building, 110 Southwark Street, London SE1 0SU (*Tel:* 020 3148 4474).

ACKOWLEDGEMENTS

Firstly thanks to Michael Hall who began this series and to all colleagues, past and present, at *Country Life*, who make this work possible; to Camilla Costello and Justin Hobson, *Country Life* Picture Librarians and their assistants, especially Helen Carey and Paula Fahey; to Piers Burnett and Bill McCreadie at Aurum Press; to Clare Howell for her supportive and intelligent editing and James Campus for his consistently wonderful designs; also to Susannah Glynn and to Sue Palmer for their editorial assistance; to Paul Barker, photographer, for his brilliant modern interpretations of these buildings for *Country Life*, and all the photographers who have been before him, named and unnamed.

Also I have to express warmest thanks to numerous friends and colleagues for advice and inspiration and support, especially John and Eileen Harris, Leslie Geddes-Brown, William Palin, Steve Parissien, Tim Richardson, Christopher Ridgway and David Watkin who all gave generous advice; and to others, including Clive Aslet, Jean Christie, Sir Howard Colvin, Milly Cumming, John Goodall, Mark Hedges, John Lord, Mary Miers, Tim Mowl, Octavia Pollock, John Martin Robinson, Frank Salmon, Caroline Scott, the late Giles Worsley, and Lucy Worsley.

I would also like to thank the owners of the houses, and those connected with their care, especially Ray Biggs, Nick Cox, John Foster, John Hardy, the late Lord Hastings, the Hon. and Mrs Simon Howard, John Hoy, His Grace the Duke of Marlborough, Mr and Mrs Seymour, Richard Wheeler and Lady Willoughby de Eresby; and, of course, I would like to express my enormous debt to the invaluable books and essays by the senior Vanbrugh scholars, especially Geoffrey Beard, Kerry Downes, Vaughan Hart and Robert Williams; also I would like to record my thanks to the librarians of Cambridge University Library and the library of the Department of History of Art, and especially the team at the London Library.

And, finally, thanks to my wife Sophie and our daughters, Georgia and Miranda, who are, all three, the light of my life.

LIST OF ARTICLES

This is a list of the primary articles in *Country Life* from which the photographs reproduced in this book are principally drawn; additional photographs were taken for the articles in the 1920s, which were used in *In English Homes, Period IV, Vol II: The Work of Sir John Vanbrugh and His School, 1699–1736*, published in 1928. The name of the author is given first; the photographer's name is given in brackets, where known.

'The Bicentenary of Sir John Vanbrugh', 20 March 1926, H. Avray Tipping.
Blenheim Palace, Oxfordshire, 29 May and 5 June 1909, H. Avray Tipping.
'Blenheim Revisited: Grinling Gibbons at Blenheim', 20 May 1949, David Green; (F. W. Westley).
'Blenheim: Architecture of Albion', 9 October 2003, Giles Worsley; (Paul Barker).
'Treasures for Blenheim's hero', 22 July 2004, Charles Avery; (Paul Barker).
Claremont, Surrey, 21 January 1928, H. Avray Tipping; (Arthur Gill).
'Newly Discovered Vanbrugh's Design for Claremont', 25 February 1949, Laurence Whistler.
'The Kit-Cat at Claremont', 17 November 2005, Tim Richardson; (Clive Boursnell).
Castle Howard, Yorkshire, 13 February 1904.
Castle Howard, Yorkshire, 4, 11 and 25 June 1927, H. Avray Tipping; (A. E. Henson).
'Outworks of Castle Howard', 6 and 13 August 1927, H. Avray Tipping; (A. E. Henson).
'The Evolution of Castle Howard', 30 January 1953, Laurence Whistler.
'In the English Campagna', 27 September 2001, Giles Worsley; (Paul Barker).
'A Dome for All Seasons: Castle Howard', 1 April 1999, Christopher Ridgway; (Tim Imrie-Tait).
Grimsthorpe Castle, Lincolnshire, 2 August 1903.
Grimsthorpe Castle, Lincolnshire, 12, 19, and 26 April 1924, Christopher Hussey; (A. E. Henson).
Grimsthorpe Castle, Lincolnshire, 26 November and 3 December 1987, Gervase Jackson-Stops; (Jonathan Gibson).
Grimsthorpe Castle, Lincolnshire, 17 April 2008, Jeremy Musson; (Paul Barker).
Kimbolton Castle, Huntingdonshire, 23 and 30 September 1911, H. Avray Tipping.
Kimbolton Castle, Huntingdonshire, 5, 12, 19 and 26 December 1968, Arthur Oswald; (Jonathan Gibson).
Kimbolton Castle, Cambridgeshire, 30 March 2006, Simon Thurley; (Paul Barker).
Kings Weston, Gloucestershire, 11 November 1899, (F. W. Westley).
Kings Weston, Gloucestershire, 30 April 1927 Christopher Hussey; (F. W. Westley).
'Mylne and Kings Weston', 23 January 1953, Christopher Gotch; (F. W. Westley).
Lumley Castle, Co. Durham, 18 June 1910, W. H. St John Hope.
Queen Anne's Orangery at Kensington Palace, 29 January 1927, H. Avray Tipping (A. E. Henson).
Seaton Delaval Hall, Northumberland, 8 and 15 December 1923, Christopher Hussey; (A. E. Henson).
Seaton Delaval Hall, Northumberland, 6 November 2003, Jeremy Musson; (Paul Barker).
Stowe House, Buckinghamshire, 27 March 2003, Giles Worsley; (Paul Barker).
Stowe, Buckinghamshire, 'Vanbrugh and the Spirit of Rome', 27 September 2001, Giles Worsley; (Paul Barker).
'Vanbrugh's work at Stowe House, Buckinghamshire', 19 February 1959, Laurence Whistler.

CONTENTS

*

Introduction 6

CASTLE HOWARD, silhouetted against the half-light of the dawn or dusk, is one of the great sights of English architecture. It is astonishing to think that this vast, dream-like house, designed in 1699, was the first major work of a complete novice – John Vanbrugh (1664–1726). At the age of thirty-five, after an already varied career as merchant, soldier and playwright of national fame, Vanbrugh turned his hand to architecture, first creating this bold and original conception and then the mighty palace of Blenheim, two of the great iconic houses of their age – indeed of any age. There is something very English in the way heroic imagination and pragmatism met in the amiable character and magnificent architecture of Sir John Vanbrugh. From his surprise beginnings as a gentleman amateur, he provided the otherwise restrained English Baroque age with some of its most glorious and memorable country houses.

From what we may know of any man from another age to our own, Vanbrugh seems a likeable character: imaginative, witty, and adventurous. He left no personal memoir, but his numerous letters teem with intuition, experience, intelligence and friendship. And indeed, his gift for language played a central part in his life, both as a playwright and as an architect, able to articulate his views and design vision engagingly and persuasively. Visiting his houses, reading his letters, and inspecting his surviving drawings and designs, I have found my admiration growing for this original and quick-witted character.

Some sense of his personality lies in the introductory memoir in the account given by his friend, the popular actor, Colley Cibber: 'Sir John Vanbrugh's pen is to be not a little to be admir'd for its Spirit, Ease and Readiness in producing Plays so fast upon the Neck of one another; for notwithstanding this quick Dispatch, there is a clear and lively Simplicity in his Wit, that neither wants the Ornaments of learning, nor has the least Smell of the Lamp in it.'

Cibber continued: 'As the Face of a fine Woman, with only her Locks loose, about her, may be then in its greatest Beauty, such were his Productions, only adorn'd by Nature … And indeed his Wit, and Humour, was so little laboured, that his most entertaining Scenes seem'd to be no more, than his common Conversation committed to Paper … As his conceptions were so full of Life and Humour, it is not much to be wondered at.'

Kerry Downes's wide-ranging *Sir John Vanbrugh: A Biography* (1987) reinforces the impression that he was a man who it would have been a pleasure to know. A good companion, clubbable and funny, sensitive and capable of bringing meaning out of an idea, making dreams a reality, but no fool. Active and literary, he was also hard working and business orientated. In politics, he was a Whig, associated with the ambitions of that party, for which the principal rallying point was the championing of the Protestant succession and the constitutional limitation of the powers of the crown. He was a useful ally to influential Whigs, many of them experienced military commanders and politicians, part of the rising new nobility, and his letters are full of political gossip and acute observations.

Vanbrugh's own reliance on his familial and political networks illustrates something of the political uncertainties of the time or, at least, the rapidly changing political landscape: from the arrival of an invited usurper, William, with his Stuart-born wife, Mary, in 1688, to the inheritance by the last legitimate Stuart heir, Queen Anne, in 1702, to the peaceful accession of the first Hanover, King George I in 1714. Vanbrugh served the two latter monarchs directly in his role as Comptroller of the Queen's (then of the King's) Works, responsible for royal palaces and related projects. This was a world in which personal contact and individual patronage were essential.

Vanbrugh's imagination and his ability to communicate, as shown in his numerous letters to friends and most importantly to patrons, the shimmer of his ideas and confidence, are evident from the start. His easy way with words is shown in two letters written to his patron and close friend, Thomas Pelham-Holles, Earl of Clare, who became the 1st Duke of Newcastle. On 15 September 1720, he wrote that he did not want the 1st Duke of Chandos to see the great hall that was being built at Claremont for Lord Clare until it was completed, so 'that it may Stair in his face, And knock him downe at Once.' In another letter, encouraging him to take Nottingham Castle as one of his principal seats, he wrote: 'I cannot but think you will extreamly like [it] when a little used to it. At first, perhaps, you'll

Castle Howard, Yorkshire, designed in 1699, was Vanbrugh's first major work, seen from the south, with its distinctive silhouette. It was the first English country house to be crowned by a substantial dome.

think it Stairs you in the face wth a pretty Impudent countenance.'

It is a memorable phrase that could well apply to a number of Vanbrugh's own buildings and illustrates his acute consideration of how a building was seen, and even of the 'personality' it might have. It is true that not everyone loves Vanbrugh's architecture but throughout the twentieth century, artists, poets and historians can be found to be marvelling at his work, straining to find the right words, as his buildings somehow defy the normal conventions of description and call for a theasaurus of superlatives: bold, monumental, ingenious, unexpected.

Yet, Vanbrugh's reputation also suffered a sudden eclipse, even in his own lifetime. The young architectural bloods were snapping at his heels. Horace Walpole said Vanbrugh and the Palladian amateur, Sir Thomas Robinson, stood spitting and swearing at each other when they met at Castle Howard. The other two best-known architects of the English Baroque, Sir Christopher Wren and Nicholas Hawksmoor, suffered from the same critics and confounders. Vanbrugh's houses have their faults, as all buildings do, but they were sidelined essentially for their originality.

The new generation were dedicated followers of Lord Burlington, and thus of his canonical heroes: the sixteenth-century Italian architect Andrea Palladio who designed the famous villas in the Veneto for the Venetian aristocracy, and Inigo Jones, the court architect to Charles I, who was incidentally first a designer of masques and entertainments. They rejected the freer and undoubtedly more original interpretation of the Classical models we associate with Vanbrugh and

Hawksmoor, his collaborator at Castle Howard and Blenheim and designer of a series of remarkable London churches, including Christ Church, Spitalfields. This was despite Vanbrugh's and Hawksmoor's obvious interest in and admiration for Palladio and antique sources.

To appreciate the character of Vanbrugh we should look at the most famous portrait of him, painted by Sir Godfrey Kneller BT. *c.*1704–10, now in the National Portrait Gallery. This is genuinely a documentary source for his architectural career. It was painted as one of a set of portraits of the members of the Kit-Cat Club, which had been established by the London bookseller, Jacob Tonson, in the 1690s, and originally met in the tavern at Temple Bar kept by Christopher Catling. Essentially a political society, it included several of Vanbrugh's clients, among them Charles Howard, 3rd Earl of Carlisle, who commissioned Castle Howard, and John Churchill, 1st Duke of Marlborough, patron of Blenheim.

Politically they were mostly Whigs, who saw themselves as the champions of British liberties. Horace Walpole observed in his *Anecdotes of Painting* (1765) that the Kit-Cat Club was 'generally mentioned as a set of wits, in reality the patriots that saved Britain'. In Kneller's portrait, Vanbrugh holds dividers in his hands, the well-established attribute of the architect.

Vanbrugh also wears a medal denoting the high heraldic office he held as Clarenceux King of Arms, the second senior officer at the

Above: *Sir John Vanbrugh painted by Sir Godfrey Kneller Bt., around 1710, wearing the medal of his heraldic office and holding the dividers of an architect.*

Left: *The north portico at Stowe, Buckinghamshire, probably designed by Vanbrugh in around 1720 for Lord Cobham, as an addition to the existing house.*

College of Arms, appointed by the sovereign. He was promoted to this post in 1704 as a result of Lord Carlisle's patronage, which other established heralds grumbled at, but which gave him a hand in creating the image of nobility that is so evident in his architecture. It also gave him a role in major state occasions in which to indulge his sense of theatre – although in 1725, he said in reference to his post that it was 'got in jest'.

Vanbrugh's conversion to a career in architecture seems to have been sudden. Lord Carlisle played the decisive role, commissioning him to build his first great house, Castle Howard, from 1699, after his initial and unsatisfactory period of time with William Talman, the talented but high-handed architect of the south front of Chatsworth. The historian, Margaret Whinney, wrote about Talman in the *Journal of the Warburg and Courtauld Institutes* in 1955: 'he was a disagreeable draughtsman, and a singularly unattractive man. Indeed his avarice and conceit make the study of his work peculiarly difficult, since he quarrelled with almost all his clients.' The reputation of Castle Howard and Vanbrugh's appointment (again as a result of Carlisle's patronage) to the prestigious role of Comptroller of the Queen's Works led directly to his commission to design Blenheim, on which work began in 1705 – a project of yet more national prestige.

Although Vanbrugh's early interest in architecture remains invisible to history, it is difficult to imagine that he came entirely unprepared for his role as an architect. It seems likely that he had some background in Classical texts or the theory of architecture in treatise form, if not much practical design experience. By 1701, he had also designed a small house for himself, a remarkable little building amid the ruins of Whitehall Palace, which had burnt down in 1698, of which, the Banqueting House, one of the great masterpieces of Inigo Jones, is the only building to survive.

Sir Christopher Wren, the Surveyor of the King's Works, had had hopes of being asked to rebuild the royal palace, and was surprised to find permission given for a private house on the site. Vanbrugh's quirky little house was two storeys high, above a raised basement, within a centrepiece of a rusticated arcade; the first-storey arcade gave on to a wrought-iron balcony.

Vanbrugh added wings eleven years later, with Venetian windows, known as Serliana, in a much more Palladian spirit (Giles Worsley suggested that they were modelled on Palladio's Villa Pogliano). But in the first form this remarkable little house must have seemed elaborate for its diminutive size. It may well have originally been planned as a showpiece both of Vanbrugh's presence on the architectural scene and his ability to produce grandeur even on this modest scale.

This was the house that inspired the savage satire of the Tory clergyman, wit and poet, Dean Jonathan Swift. In his poem *Built from the ruins of Whitehall that was burnt*, 1703, he mocked Vanbrugh and his creation, describing the building as 'a thing resembling a goose-pie'. It was known as Goose Pie House thereafter, although long since demolished. Fortunately, it is recorded in a watercolour drawing prepared by pupils in John Soane's office for his Royal Academy lecture on 16 March 1815, and now in the collections of Sir John Soane's Museum.

In another version of the poem, *The History of Vanbrug's house* (published in 1706), Swift famously wrote: 'Van's Genius without Thought or Lecture/Is hugely turn'd to architecture', imagining that Vanbrugh, having watched some boys making houses out of mud, decided he could do better:

> From such deep rudiments as these,
> Van is become, by due degrees,
> For building famed and justly reckon'd,
> At court, Vitruvius the Second.

In 1710, Swift described meeting Vanbrugh in a letter to Stella (his private name for Esther Johnson, a young woman whose education he had supervised): 'I dined to-day at Sir Richard Temple's, with Congreve, Vanbrugh, Lieutenant-General Farrington, etc. Vanbrugh, I believe I told you, had a long quarrel with me about those Verses on his House; but we were very civil and cold. Lady Marlborough used

to teaze him with them, which had made him angry, though he be a good-natured fellow.'

Swift's earlier verses also included a reference to Vanbrugh's role as a herald:

> Van (for 'tis fit the Reader know it)
> Is both a Herald and a Poet;
> No wonder then, if nicely skill'd
> in each Capacity to Build.
> An herald, he can in a Day
> Repair a House gone to decay;
> Or by Atchievements, Arms, Device,
> Erect a new one in a Trice.

Intriguingly, Vaughan Hart raised in *History Today* (July 1992) the idea that Vanbrugh may have been the inspiration for Swift's Gulliver in *Gulliver's Travels*.

But did Vanbrugh really turn to architecture without 'Thought or Lecture', by which Swift presumably meant study? Vanbrugh had begun working closely with Hawksmoor from 1700 and was soon

using Palladio's *Quattro Libri I* as a venerated source. A letter to his friend Jacob Tonson, dated 13 July 1703, refers to: 'The book you mention wch I wanted, you'll oblige me to get. Tis Palladio in French, wth the Plans of most of the Houses he built; there is one without the Plans, but Tis that with em I would have.' This is thought to have been Roland Fréart's 1650 French edition of Palladio. He certainly later used it practically, as it is mentioned as left behind at Blenheim in a letter of 1711.

But was there other evidence of architectural experience or training before 1699? John Vanbrugh was of well-connected merchant stock. His grandfather, Gillis, had fled to London from Haarlem in 1616 to escape religious persecution as a Protestant – their surname was often rendered Vanbrug, Van Brugg or Vanbrook or Vanbrooke.

Vanbrugh's father, Giles, was a successful London cloth merchant. They lived in London before moving to Chester, where he is said to have had an entrepreneurial finger in many pies, including property and the grain and sugar trade (although he was probably not the 'sugar-baker' that he has traditionally been described as).

While Giles Vanbrugh was clearly a hard-nosed man of commerce, he had been brought up a gentleman and was a man of some culture. In a bizarre letter of 1678 to Henry Compton, Bishop of London, proposing that they should send a force to capture the Vatican library as a rebuff to Papist intrigue, Giles mentions that as part of his travels in France and Italy in 1655–58, he had spent a year in Rome for his education. This surely raises interesting questions about what experience and understanding of the architecture of Rome, or library of material he may have imparted to his oldest surviving son.

There is also a touching aside in a letter written by Vanbrugh to Lord Carlisle on 17 July 1722 regarding his young son: 'I fancy your Lordships Godson will be a Professor that way, for he knows Pillars, & Arches and Round Windows & Square Windows already, whether he finds them in a Book or in the Streets', which may possibly reflect Vanbrugh's own early study or exposure to architectural ideas.

John Vanbrugh's mother, Elizabeth Carleton, was of aristocratic birth. She was the daughter of Sir Dudley Carleton of Imber Court, Surrey, who had inherited his estate from his distinguished and cultivated uncle, also Sir Dudley, later Viscount Dorchester, who was James I's Ambassador to Venice (during which time he escorted the Earl of Arundel and Inigo Jones around the city) and later Ambassador to Paris.

Vanbrugh's first steps into adult working life were in commerce. In 1681, he worked in the wine trade but by 1682 he entered the service of the East India Company, and, astonishingly, in 1683, he sailed for Surat, in the Gujarat region of India, where he worked for a year before returning to London (as was recently discovered by architectural historian, Robert Williams, and published in 2000 in *Sir John Vanbrugh and Landscape Architecture in Baroque England, 1690–1730*).

He left no account of his time there, nor did he ever refer to it in his riveting letters. But this does mean that Vanbrugh was the only major English architect of his day who had had any first-hand experience of India. While the influence of his Indian experiences is

not perhaps immediately apparent in his work, Mr Williams has identified one of Vanbrugh's sketches as loosely based on the Anglo-Indian cemetery at Surat and suggests that this experience was the basis for the fashion of freestanding mausolea in English country parks.

This sketch was drawn in 1711 to accompany Vanbrugh's elegantly written 'proposals about Building ye New Churches' (a manuscript now in the Bodleian Library) in which he referred to the creation of cemeteries outside the city: 'If these Caemitarys be consecrated, Handsomely and regularly wall'd in, and planted with Trees in such form as to make a Solemn distinction between one Part and another'; he hoped that people would build in them, 'Lofty and Noble mausoleums erected over them in Freestone.'

Mr Williams also suggests that Vanbrugh's exposure to the scale

and quality of Mughal architecture in Gujarat, so memorable for the scale of its palaces and temples dominating the landscape, was a spur to his later invention as a designer. Perhaps indeed, it was a spur to his very interest in architecture.

One touching account of the young Vanbrugh's return home was given by his East India Company boss, John Child, quoted by Mr Williams, noting that John Vanbrugh and Robert Graham took their passage for England: 'being quite weary of these parts, & in bigg expectation of much sooner raiseing theire fortunes in England depending on theire good friends to put ym into places of great profit, Credt and ease, they are a Couple of young men, very fitt for business … we heartily wish ym both well.'

On his return, having used up his father's business contacts for a career, Vanbrugh turned to the aristocratic connections of his mother. Her kinsman, Theophilus Hastings, 7th Earl of Huntingdon, got him a commission in his own regiment. Finding himself serving with Catholic officers, Vanbrugh resigned and transferred himself to the household of another of his mother's kinsmen, James Bertie, 1st Earl of Abingdon, alongside three cousins, including the sons of the

Earl of Lindsey – Robert Bertie, who later became 1st Duke of Ancaster and Kesteven, and who was Vanbrugh's initial patron at Grimsthorpe, and his younger brother, Peregrine Bertie, later 1st Baron Willoughby.

How his poor mother must have fretted at his next twist of fortune. In 1688, travelling in France with Robert Bertie, Vanbrugh apparently praised William of Orange in public, then newly at war with France. He was arrested (probably more for hostage value than for his actual offence) and held first in Calais, then in 1691 in the Château de Vincennes, and in 1692 was transferred to the Bastille.

Later that year he was released on parole, apparently enjoying some weeks to see Paris before being returned to England, a time possibly to have noted the quality of the magnificent architecture of late-seventeenth-century Paris, such as the Collège des Quatre Nations. When Christopher Wren visited important new buildings in Paris in 1665, he famously wrote to a friend: 'that I might not lose the Impressions of them, I shall bring you almost all France in paper.' Perhaps Vanbrugh brought back almost all Paris in his memory and imagination. He read and spoke French and one could speculate

about the titles or engravings that might have come his way while at Vincennes or the Bastille, where he was kept in a comfortable confinement befitting his rank.

Peregrine Bertie secured Vanbrugh a minor sinecure as one of the auditors of the Duchy of Lancaster, which he held until 1702. But he also returned immediately to military service in 1694. He served under the command of another relation, Sir Thomas Osborne, Marquess of Carmarthen (previously Earl of Danby and later 1st Duke of Leeds), who mentioned Vanbrugh in his *Journal of the Brest-Expedition* (published in 1694), praising his courage and saying that 'in a great many things [he] was extremely serviceable both by his advice and otherwise.' In 1695, Vanbrugh was commissioned as a captain of marines under Lord Berkeley.

During his time in prison, and perhaps before, Vanbrugh appears to have contemplated writing for the theatre. Before he had left the marines in 1698, he had managed to pull of the first real (national) success of his life by becoming a playwright. In 1696, his hugely successful comedy *The Relapse: or Virtue in Danger* was performed at the Drury Lane Theatre. Horace Walpole in an essay 'Thoughts on

Comedy', written in the 1770s, observed that Vanbrugh was reputed 'the best writer of dialogue that we have seen' and that he 'exactly hit the style, manners, and character of his contemporaries.'

The Relapse was a sequel to Colley Cibber's *Love's Last Shift*, from which Vanbrugh carried over the character, Sir Novelty Fashion, whom he elevated to the peerage as Lord Foppington, described by another character in the play as arriving 'with two coaches and six horses, twenty footmen and pages, a coat worth four score pounds, and a periwig down to his knees.'

It was a hit and made Vanbrugh's name overnight, although this and his other wholly original play *The Provok'd Wife*, first performed in 1697, were attacked in 1698 by Jeremy Collier in his *Short View of the Immorality and Profaneness of the English Stage*. But the knockabout humour and teasing of social convention in these comedies made Vanbrugh the man of the hour, and probably brought him to the attention of the crew who formed the Kit-Cat Club. Vanbrugh also translated two French plays, *Aesop* (1697) and the tantalisingly named *The Country House* (concerning a man's inability to put off unwanted guests), first performed in 1703.

Vanburgh's experience as a playwright and theatrical entrepreneur meant that he not only had a vivid awareness of the theatrical effect of action on stage, but also of the latest in stage machinery and scenography. As Frank McCormick pointed out in *Sir John Vanbrugh: the Playwright as Architect* (1991) what 'contemporary scene designers accomplished with wings and shutters and arched borders, Vanbrugh accomplished through the use of arches, columns, corridors and wings.'

Play of perspective was the key and Vanbrugh's awareness of the observer in his designs, of the views from within and without his

creations. As McCormick noted, everyone who has visited any of Vanbrugh's houses 'will recall … instances of Vanbrugh's artful direction of the viewer's gaze toward a figurative stage.'

Tim Mowl in his essay 'Antiquaries, Theatre and Early Medievalism' (*Sir John Vanbrugh and Landscape Architecture in Baroque England, 1690–1730*) goes further and explores the imagery of Restoration theatre and Dryden as the background of his patrons' visual awareness: 'It was this familiarity with the exotic heights of drama, added to their military successes abroad, that allowed the triumphant Whigs – Carlisle, Marlborough, Manchester – to accept impossible palaces as no more than their due. They could take romantic grandiosity in their stride.'

The Queen's Theatre (later known as The King's), which Vanbrugh designed in the Haymarket in 1704–05 while simultaneously working on Blenheim, was thought to be a very fine piece of architecture. Daniel Defoe described it as a French church, although as Cibber put it: 'every proper contrivance of a good Theatre had been sacrificed to shew the Audience a vast triumphal Piece of Architecture, in which by means of the Spaciousness of the Dome, voices could not be successfully represented', as the actors voices were lost. Vanbrugh did not prosper as a theatrical impresario of drama and Italian opera, and by 1708 when he sold his theatre business, his architectural career was becoming more serious.

For by this time, a new chapter had begun. Earlier, in 1702, Vanbrugh had been rewarded by his patron Lord Carlisle – then at the brief peak of his political influence and for a short time Lord Treasurer, the highest office in the land. He secured Vanbrugh's appointment as Comptroller of The Queen's Works, in place of his gifted but unhappy rival William Talman, and in the service of the Surveyor, Sir Christopher Wren.

In an illustration of the fickle and political nature of appointments in architecture, a decade later, in 1713, Vanbrugh was deprived of his comptrollership, ostensibly on the basis of an unwise letter in which he criticised the Tory administration and the Queen. He was, however, restored in 1715 by King George I, at the Duke of

Above: *Burley on the Hill, Rutland, built for the 2nd Earl of Nottingham in the 1690s, and one of the houses visited by Vanbrugh as he prepared to design Castle Howard.*

Left: *The 1680s south front of Chatsworth, Derbyshire, designed by William Talman for the 1st Duke of Devonshire.*

Above right: *A Vanbrugh palace in miniature: the 1720s kitchen wing of Seaton Delaval Hall, Northumberland.*

Marlborough's intervention, when he also became Surveyor of the Royal Gardens and Waters. He became Surveyor to Greenwich Hospital in 1716.

As Comptroller in 1702, Vanbrugh was one of the most powerful men in British architecture, second only to Wren. He seems to have been an efficient and conscientious administrator. His relationship with Sir Christopher Wren was possibly strained when he challenged the practice of members of the Works (such as masons and carpenters) undertaking royal contracts – a system which while not desirable, Wren was inclined to overlook as it had served the Works well enough for many years.

Vanbrugh brought things to a head with the Lord Treasurer, who supported his position. However, when in 1718 he was surprisingly

passed over for the role of Surveyor in favour of William Benson, Vanbrugh wistfully wrote a friend to say that he might have had Wren's job in 1715, 'but refus'd it, out of Tenderness for Sr Ch: Wren'.

Vanbrugh certainly showed tenderness to his workmen, fretting about the effect of non-payment of bills on them during the crisis period of construction of Blenheim. He also championed and protected Hawksmoor, making him his own deputy when in 1718 he was deprived of his role at the King's Works, in yet another politically motivated reshuffle of positions.

In 1721, Vanbrugh wrote to his friend Brigadier Watkins: 'Poor Hawskmoor, What a Barbarous Age, have his fine, ingenious Parts fallen into. What wou'd Monsrr: Colbert in France have given for Such a Man?' (Louis XIV's First Minister). But about rivals or people he considered upstarts he could be crushing, as he famously wrote the same year of his humbly born but fast-rising colleague, Thomas Ripley: 'When I met with his Name (and Esquire to it) in the Newspaper; such a laugh came upon me, I had like to Beshit myself.'

Vanbrugh seems to have contributed relatively little as original designer to any of the royal projects which came under his care, except a new kitchen at St James's Palace and fitting out an apart-

ment for the Prince of Wales at Hampton Court. The kitchen at St James's survives with an unexpectedly grand interior with a high cove and clerestory. Like Ledoux and Cockerell, Vanbrugh would leave his mark on any building however humble.

The red-brick Orangery, or eating house, built at Kensington Palace during Queen Anne's reign and long attributed to Vanbrugh is now given by most historians to Hawksmoor as designer. Vanbrugh did design a characteristically tapered water tower there in 1722–24, with crenellations, long since demolished.

He tried to interest King George I in more ambitious proposals for Hampton Court, with a new open courtyard of lodgings framing the great hall, but to no avail. The great hall was converted to a theatre in 1718, and Kerry Downes suggests in *Sir John Vanbrugh: A Biography* (1987) that while Thornhill was in charge of scenery, Vanbrugh was probably the architect. In 1711, he was made Commissioner for the Building of Fifty New Churches in London, of which Hawksmoor was the surveyor and designer of several. Vanbrugh made proposals but none were commissioned.

Vanbrugh's career as a private architect was also busy and demanding. He was appointed architect to Castle Howard in 1699 and the house (although one wing was not finished at his death) was largely complete by 1712: a vast-seeming palace complex, topped by a great dome (the first on an English country house), carefully sited and extended with a deep kitchen court that increased both its outline and profile.

At Blenheim, Vanbrugh was officially appointed in 1705, and resigned in 1716, when years of bitter litigation and wrangling with the intelligent but mean-spirited Duchess of Marlborough followed, and the building was not largely complete until 1725. Even then only one of the two proposed service courts was successfully completed. Blenheim was not just vast-seeming but a truly gigantic palace structure, inspired by Castle Howard but overlaid with the spirit of Versailles.

Perhaps he was also drawing on his knowledge of great English architecture of the preceding centuries. There are echoes of four-teenth-century castles and of the prodigy houses of the sixteenth century, such as Wollaton and Longleat, in Vanbrugh's reach for greatness in these houses. Tim Mowl has cited Vanbrugh's 'muted medievalism' and 'a longstanding tradition in English architectural design not just of conservatism, but of obstinate insularity and deliberate historicism.'

Vanbrugh's documented domestic work includes the remodelling of Kimbolton Castle for the 4th Earl of Manchester, 1707–10, and a country retreat for himself, Chargate, near Esher, Surrey, in 1709–10. He sold the house in 1715 to Thomas Pelham-Holles, the Earl of Clare (later 1st Duke of Newcastle), and extended it for him into a magnificent pile, renamed Claremont.

In 1718–20, Vanbrugh created a new retreat for himself on a hill overlooking Greenwich, known as Vanbrugh Castle, designing houses nearby for his family – Mince Pie House, for a brother, and another, The Nunnery, for his unmarried sisters. He had to extend his own

Top: *The Kensington Palace Orangery, from the south, built in 1704 with Vanbrugh's involvement, but thought to be a design by Hawksmoor. It was used as a summer dining room.*

Above: *The bold centrepiece of the Orangery, with its distinctive articulation of parts.*

Left: *Easton Neston, Northamptonshire, designed by Nicholas Hawksmoor and begun in around 1695.*

little castle after taking, in his early fifties, what he called in a letter to Jacob Tonson of 1 July 1719, that 'great Leap in the Dark, Marriage'. He had married six months before, Henrietta Maria, a young widow, and daughter of Colonel James Yarburgh of Heslington Hall in Yorkshire. They had a son Charles in October 1720, and a second son, who died young in 1723.

In 1718, Vanbrugh also began work on Eastbury in Dorset – his largest house after Blenheim and Castle Howard – for George Dodington, a cousin of Richard Temple, 1st Viscount Cobham (who had served under Marlborough). Vanbrugh designed numerous temples for Cobham's gardens at Stowe in these years, working closely with Charles Bridgeman, the great landscape gardener. He also made various alterations and additions to the house, including the principal north portico and the orangery.

For wealthy Admiral George Delaval, who admired Vanbrugh's work at Castle Howard, he designed and built a new country seat for an old family estate – Seaton Delaval Hall, begun 1721 and completed in 1728. For his cousin and childhood friend, Robert Bertie, he drew up designs in around 1715 for the improvement of the family home at Grimsthorpe Castle, Lincolnshire, which were put into action by his son in 1723. Even though only partly realised, they resulted in one of

the most sublime of his great entrance fronts which, like Seaton Delaval, seems to combine some flavour of castle with a fantasy element of the Classical tradition.

For Vanbrugh, these great private commissions stand alongside his important public offices. It is thought by many authors that Vanbrugh was involved in the design of various Board of Ordnance buildings, such as the Board Room for the Woolwich Arsenal, and other buildings such as the gateway to the Royal Dockyards at Chatham, although his contribution here is not clearly documented.

Vanbrugh worked in London for Sir Robert Walpole, at Walpole House in Chelsea, and was consulted by numerous other grandees, such as the 1st Duke of Chandos at Cannons in Middlesex, and Lord Hervey at Ickworth House in Suffolk, and drew up a scheme for the 1st Earl of Cholmondley for Cholmondley Castle, his seat in Cheshire. Although nothing seems to have been built from these discussions, one can imagine numerous other consultations from the clubbable Captain Vanbrugh.

There were many smaller schemes that he explored on paper – many of which are preserved in the Elton Hall album, now held at the Victoria and Albert Museum – full of freshness and vitality and imagination, and mostly representing architectural ideas; although only a few of these can be identified with actual buildings.

Vanbrugh's work did not conform to the Palladian rulebooks and therefore he and his works suffered in reputation after his death. He had by the 1720s, in fact, begun to engage with the new formal Palladian manner, and all his major buildings were included in the arch-Palladian Colen Campbell's *Vitruvius Britannicus* (1715–25). But then Vanbrugh's buildings could scarcely be overlooked, for their scale at least. Campbell's introduction at the same time famously and deliberately condemned the 'licentious' excesses of Baroque design.

A typical Palladian critique of Vanbrugh was given by one John Dodd, who wrote in his 1735 *A Tour through England*, of Blenheim that: 'its Beauties, & Absurdities are so blended, that while you are expatiating upon one, you are checked by the intervening Ideas of the other ... who can admire the Largeness and Magnificence of the House, and not Deplore, the absence of Beauty and Taste from this Place?'

But Vanbrugh's star never entirely waned. He had his later eighteenth-century admirers amongst Neo-Classical architects, such as Robert and James Adam, who mentioned him in the introduction to their *Works in Architecture* (1778). He was, they said: 'a great man, whose reputation as an architect has long been carried down the stream by a torrent of undistinguishing prejudice and abuse. Sir John Vanbrugh's genius was of the first class and in point of movement, novelty and ingenuity, his works have not been exceeded by anything in modern times.'

But their praise was tempered: 'unluckily for the reputation of this excellent artist, his taste kept no pace with his genius, and his works

Blenheim Palace, Oxfordshire, looking from the portico towards the kitchen court; photographed in 1909.

are so crowded with barbarisms and absurdities, and so borne down by their own preposterous weight, that none but the discerning can seperate their merits from their defects.'

Robert Adam also wrote that: 'Vanbrugh understood better than both [Inigo Jones and Wren] the art of living among the great. A commodious arrangement of apartments was therefore his peculiar merit.' And remarkably, it has been suggested by Michel Gallet that the great French Neo-Classical architect, Claude-Nicolas Ledoux, admired and visited Vanbrugh's buildings.

Vanbrugh was also admired by Sir Joshua Reynolds, although he may also have seen him as a Whig hero. Reynolds referred to him in his *Discourse XIII*, 1786, one of his lectures to Royal Academy students, as follows: 'To speak ... of Vanbrugh in the language of a Painter, he had originality of invention, he understood light and shadow, and had great skill in composition ... He perfectly under-

Above: Vanbrughian arcading of the surviving wing at Eastbury Park in Dorset, built for George Dodington from 1718.

Left: A Vanbrughian arch: a corner of the main room in Vanbrugh Castle, the house that he built for himself overlooking Greenwich, from 1718.

stood in his art what is most difficult in ours; the conduct of the background; by which the design and invention is set off to the greatest advantage.'

The great Sir John Soane, the Royal Academy's Professor of Architecture, dubbed Vanbrugh 'the Shakespeare of Architects'. In his eleventh lecture to the Academy of 16 March 1815, he asserted that Vanbrugh 'had all the fire and power of Michael Angelo and Bernini, without any of the elegant softness and classical delicacy of Palladio and his followers. The young architect ... by studying the picturesque effects of his works, will learn to think for himself and acquire a taste of his own.'

For this lecture Soane had three remarkable drawings specially prepared: the first showing Blenheim in its full glory, with the detail picked out, the second image, with a mist descending over it, so that the massing and overall composition could be better observed, and finally, just the pale outlines of the extraordinary silhouette. Undoubtedly, for Soane this illustrated the touch of a poet among architects, as it must do for anyone seeing Blenheim or Castle Howard in the early morning or late evening.

Other architects responded to Vanbrugh's architecture and

imagination, including C. R. Cockerell (designer of the Ashmolean Museum, Oxford), most notably in the arcaded chimneys of his unbuilt proposals of 1835 for the Fitzwilliam Museum, Cambridge. By the late nineteenth century, Vanbrugh had become one of the symbols of his age, both as dramatist and architect. This was part of a revival of interest in Baroque forms, and, perhaps, especially Baroque detail in Edwardian architecture, not least in the world of the London theatre.

At this time, Wren's designs for the remodelling of Hampton Court were becoming a source for a style of public architecture, neatly called 'Wrenaissance', while St Paul's, its glorious dome at the centre of the City of London, was being imitated around the Empire. From the 1890s, Baroque had become a popular inspiration for architects, such as John Belcher and Beresford Pite who designed the much admired Chartered Accountant's Hall in London. As Derek Lindstrum observed in 'Remembering Vanbrugh' (*Sir John Vanbrugh and Landscape Architecture in Baroque England, 1690–1730*): 'the Baroque style became virtually the official one for public and commercial buildings.'

The shift in national taste led to a series of articles in *Country Life*, which began as early as 1899 with an admiring article on Blenheim Palace and with another on Kings Weston, followed by one in 1903 on Grimsthorpe, and in 1904 on Castle Howard. It was perhaps also a desire by the towering figure of Avray Tipping, the first Architectural Editor of *Country Life*, an architectural patron and designer of note and in many ways one of the fathers of British architectural history, to supply an authoritative survey of the great houses of England by period.

The articles on Vanbrugh's stately houses, written by Tipping and by the young Christopher Hussey, were quickly used to form the basis of a volume in the series *In English Homes*. This glorious volume is the only one dedicated to a named architect: *In English Homes: Period IV–Vol II, The Works of Sir John Vanbrugh and His School* (1927), and must have had its origins in Tipping's bicentennial tribute to Vanbrugh, published as an article in *Country Life* on 20 March 1926. Frank McCormick's bibliographical *Sir John Vanbrugh: A Reference Guide* (1992) illustrates a sudden rise in the number of published writings on Vanbrugh's architecture in these years.

Country Life has continued to visit and revisit these buildings throughout the century, and it is its photographs, taken across the span of one hundred and ten years, that form the inspiration and source for this book. Revisiting Vanbrugh's surviving houses in the same inquisitive but celebratory spirit as Tipping and Hussey, it aims to be a visually straightforward compendium of his surviving country house work. It will have, therefore, to exclude a fuller visual account of two of his important houses, Eastbury in Dorset and Claremont in Surrey, which were both demolished in the later eighteenth century, and other demolished or unbuilt projects.

There has been considerable research and analysis of Vanbrugh and his architecture pursued over this same century by scholars, many of whom published their findings, or tested their opinions through the

medium of the weekly country house feature in *Country Life*, notably Gervase Jackson-Stops and Giles Worsley. Vanbrugh's letters were collected, edited and published in 1927 (*The Complete Works of Sir John Vanbrugh*, Vol 4), many were addressed to his architectural patrons, others to friends, such as the publisher, Jacob Tonson, and Brigadier Watkins, who was from 1717 Surveyor of the King's Private Roads.

The first major study of Vanbrugh's architecture after *In English Homes* was Laurence Whistler's *The Imagination of Vanbrugh and his Fellow Artists* (1954). Sir Howard Colvin sorted the documented attributions in his *Biographical Dictionary of British Architects 1640–1840* (1954 and subsequent editions to 2008) and his official works in the *History of the King's Works*, Vol V (1976).

Sir John Summerson, who devoted a whole chapter to Hawksmoor and Vanbrugh in *Architecture in Britain 1530–1830* (1953) wrote: 'the story of how a school which may appropriately and with some pride be called the English Baroque School emerged from Wren's work did flower into such splendid achievements as Blenheim Palace and the London churches of Queen Anne's and George I's reign, is one of the most interesting and also one of the most difficult episodes in English architectural history.' He concluded: 'The English Baroque School, for one generation, was the creation of two men, while a third [Thomas Archer] threw his talents into the pool.'

The most influential modern scholar of Vanbrugh's architecture is undoubtedly Kerry Downes, author of the principal monograph on *Vanbrugh* (1977), which includes his accounts, travels, genealogical information and previously unpublished letters, and *Sir John Vanbrugh: A Biography* (1987). Both works have marshalled the important material of Vanbrugh's life and career into edited and published form.

Vanbrugh has also been recognised as an important influence on English landscape gardening, as David Watkin noted in *The English Vision* (1982): 'Vanbrugh's large pictorial and imaginative genius as displayed at Castle Howard, at Blenheim (with Wise, Switzer and Bridgeman) and at Stowe (with Bridgeman), deployed elements of continental baroque garden design in impressive schemes which concentrated attention in an unaccustomed way on views of the existing landscape.'

Geoffrey Beard's informative volume *The Work of John Vanbrugh*, in conjunction with the photographer A. F. Kersting, appeared in 1986, while Frank McCormick's *Sir John Vanbrugh: the Playwright as Architect* (1991) links the dramatic and the design in Vanbrugh's imagination. Modern Vanbrugh studies were brought together in *Sir John Vanbrugh and Landscape Architecture in Baroque England, 1690–1730* (2000). Vaughan Hart added his original and informative investigation into the meaning and significance of Vanbrugh's architecture in *Nicholas Hawksmoor: Rebuilding Ancient Wonders* (2002) and *Sir John Vanbrugh: A Storyteller in Stone* (2008).

Vanbrugh owed an immense debt to his assistant Hawksmoor. So this may be a good point to raise that hoary old chestnut for architectural historians of who is justly called the architect of Castle Howard

and Blenheim? Just how much belongs to which hand? Is it a right or fair question to ask when late-seventeenth-century design practice did not place as high a value of individuality as we do in modern times? Much recent scholarship tends to argue that Hawksmoor's own drawings make an increasing contribution, although Hawksmoor appears always to have regarded these projects as Vanbrugh's.

But as Kerry Downes put it neatly in the *New Oxford Dictionary of National Biography* (2004): 'The relationship between Vanbrugh and Hawksmoor was initially between the Renaissance gentleman architect, engaging in a liberal art, and the practised professional, but it soon became the close partnership that produced Castle Howard and Blenheim.' And to quote Sir John Summerson, whose chapter on English Baroque in *Architecture in Britain 1530–1830* (1953) is dominated by reference to the two men: 'The truth can only be that *both* Hawksmoor *and* Vanbrugh were very exceptional men.'

It is ironic that Hawksmoor's name was made so famous by the eponymous modern novel by Peter Ackroyd (although the architect is named Dyer and the modern detective Hawksmoor) when it is surely Vanbrugh who deserved to be the subject of a string of novels. For here was a man who had travelled to India, been imprisoned in France as a suspected spy, been a successful playwright in the

Left: *Kings Weston, Gloucestershire: Vanbrugh's playful arcading of the chimneys adds a fantasy element to the otherwise austere villa design.*

Below: *The magnificent Great Hall at Grimsthorpe Castle, Lincolnshire, a reworking of an older space; photographed in 1924.*

Above: *Detail of the painted decoration in the staircase hall at Kings Weston, Gloucestershire.*

Left: *The blind arcade in the Great Hall at Grimsthorpe Castle, Lincolnshire, is filled with paintings in* grisaille *by Thornhill of English monarchs, including the portrait of George I over the chimneypiece.*

London of Pope and Walpole, played a role in introducing Italian opera to London, who walked tall with the Whig nobility, was ridiculed by Dean Jonathan Swift, and then became an architect of some of England's greatest houses. Most men would have been satisfied with only half of the life experiences that Vanbrugh packed into his busy life.

Swift and Pope published this curiously touching apologia for their teasing of Vanbrugh (Swift in numerous poems) in their joint preface to Swift's *Miscellanies in Prose and Verse* (1727). 'In regard to Two persons only we wish our Railery, though ever so tender, or Resentment, though ever so just, had not been indulged. We speak of Sir John Vanbrugh, who was a Man of Wit and Honour, and of Mr Addison.'

But as the satirists' barbed tongues remind us, Vanbrugh's houses belong to the world of battles and awkward, quickly changing high politics. Architecture played its own part in this world. On 27 July 1708, Vanbrugh wrote in a letter to a kinsman and patron, Charles Montagu, 4th Earl of Manchester: 'All the World are running Mad after Building, as far as they can reach.' Vanbrugh undoubtedly rode the crest of this building madness. His great houses, deliberately ambitious, were intended to outdo the great palaces and houses of the day, and he quickly drew into both projects the services of one of the most experienced architects of the day, Nicholas Hawksmoor.

It cannot be stressed enough that their collaboration is a key part of this story, for while Vanbrugh certainly secured the commission for these great houses and had the overall ideas, Hawksmoor not only provided much of the detailed design and management but in both cases completed the project – Castle Howard after Vanbrugh's death and Blenheim after his resignation.

Hawksmoor's contribution was, as well as being a deeply practical man of business, also perhaps that of an architectural tutor to Vanbrugh. The good captain was clearly already well read and exposed to a wide range of architecture and literature, and would have relished the chance to discuss and learn and absorb ideas from the learned and, no doubt, more widely read in architecture, Hawksmoor. There is no record of Vanbrugh's own library, but it can be assumed that he would have been quickly exposed to the resources of the library and tastes and interests of his companion architect.

Hawksmoor's extensive library is known from the sale catalogue after his death and examined in detail in Vaughan Hart's *Nicholas Hawksmoor: Rebuilding Ancient Wonders* (2002). It included editions of Vitruvius by Barbaro and Perrault, and treatises by Alberti, Serlio, Palladio, Du Cerceau, Scamozzi, as well as works by Domenico and Carlo Fontana, and other works, such as Antoine Desgodetz's, *Les édifices antiques de Rome dessinés et mesurés très exactement sur les lieux de fer* (1682). We may assume then that after 1700 Vanbrugh was familiar with just such sources.

According to Pope (published in *Life of Alexander Pope* by Owen Ruffhead in 1769) Vanbrugh 'pretended to no high scientific knowledge in the art of building.' But then again Vanbrugh felt

sufficiently authoritative to say of the possibility of Thornhill the painter becoming Surveyor of the Works, in a letter of 15 August 1719: 'Twou'd be a pleasant Joke to the World, to See a Painter made Surveyor of the Works, in Order to Save money; When all the Small knowledge or tast they ever have of it, is only in the Great expensive part, As Collumns, Arches, Bass reliefs &c which they just learn enough of, to help fill up their Pictures.'

Many of Vanbrugh's own patrons would have been familiar with the key Classical texts that were important to him and to have their own reflections to contribute on Classical literature and great architecture encountered in Europe and elsewhere. In Vanburgh's surprising story, the significance and nature of his circle of patrons and their own cultural reference and experience is the key – not least as Grand Tourists, as in the case of Charles Howard, 3rd Earl of Carlisle, with his own first-hand experience of the grandeur that was Rome. Most, indeed, were well travelled and men of action, for whom Vanbrugh's references to Pliny the Younger's villas in his writings (and mentioned by Hawksmoor in his annotated plans for the temple

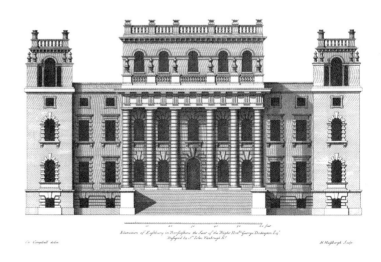

Top: *An oil painting showing Eastbury Park, Dorset as completed after Vanbrugh's death. The house was demolished in 1775.*

Above: *Engraving of the main entrance elevation for Eastbury Park, as it appeared in Vitruvius Britannicus, Vol III, 1725*

Right: *Stucco figures of the liberal arts in the main hall at Seaton Delaval Hall, Northumberland.*

a Scale of 40 feet

10   20   30   40

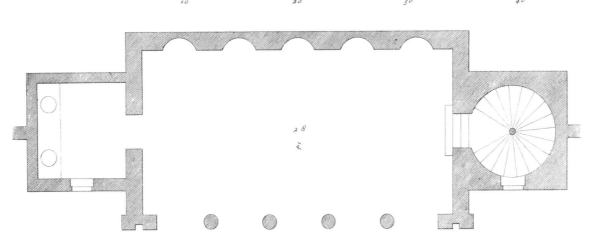

Plan and Elevation of the Bagnio in the garden at Eastbury in Dorsetshire the

Ca: Campbell delin: *Seat of the Right Honourable George Dodington Esq: Design'd by S.ʳ Iohn Vanbrugh K.ᵗ*

H.Hulsbergh Sculp:

Above: *The Bagnio, at Eastbury Park, Dorset, published in* Vitruvius Britannicus,
Vol III, 1725.

Left: *Detail of the main elevation of Eastbury Park, as depicted in*
Vitruvius Britannicus, *Vol III, 1725.*

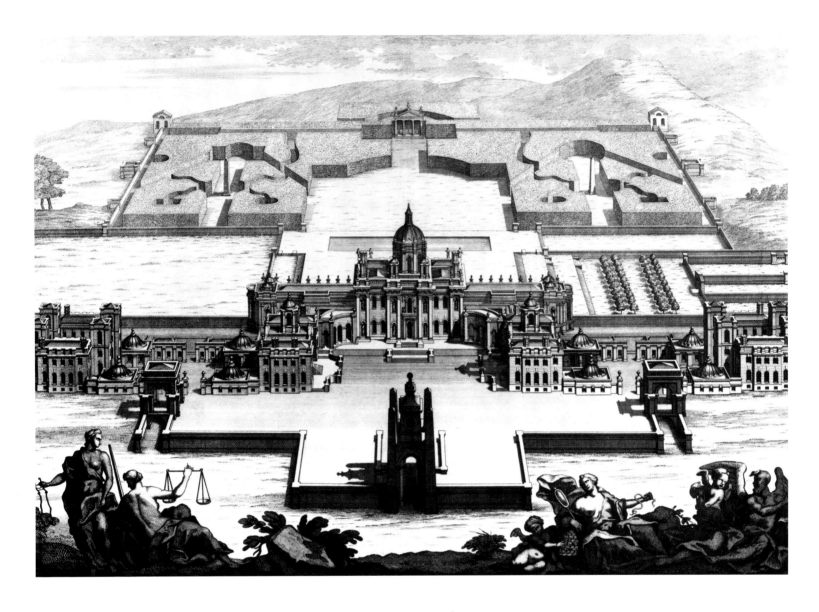

at Castle Howard) would have had resonance, with the country estate representing a symbolic retreat from the demands of public life.

Lord Manchester was Envoy to Venice, Admiral Delaval was Envoy to the King of Portugal, Edward Southwell was a Member of Parliament and senior civil servant, and from a family with long-standing links to the Grand Dukes of Tuscany, while Lord Cobham at Stowe, had also been one of Marlborough's generals. Vanbrugh surely helped them to interpret their knowledge, reading and attitudes, as well as their various experiences abroad, at home.

Vanbrugh wrote to the fiery Duchess of Marlborough on 9 June 1709 that he had prepared a 'little Picture of what had been in general propos'd to be done ... which I feard was not perfectly Understood by any explanation I had been Able to make of it by words.'

The photographs in this book, taken over the course of over a century for *Country Life* by some of the greatest photographers – from Arthur Gill, A. E. Henson to Paul Barker – are offered in the spirit of just such a sketch, allowing us to enjoy these splendours from our arm-chairs. To these I have attached this introduction and a commentary on his buildings.

Historians might write a hundred books on Vanbrugh, nothing really competes with the experience of looking at his buildings in context, or experiencing their physical presence with all their boldness and the subtle nuances of their settings. Visit them and smile at the tongue-in-cheek epitaph written by Abel Evans when Sir John Vanbrugh died on 26 March 1726: 'Lie heavy on him, Earth, for he/Laid many a heavy load on thee.'

Above: *Bird's eye view of Castle Howard, Yorkshire, published in* Vitruvius Britannicus, *Vol III, 1725, showing the full extent of the great vision of Vanbrugh and Lord Carlisle. The west wing was completed to a different design.*

Left: *The surviving cyclopean side gateway at Eastbury Park, Dorset, evocative of a Roman fortification.*

I

VANBRUGH'S FIRST
GREAT HOUSE:
CASTLE HOWARD

In 1772, Horace Walpole wrote of his first sight of Castle Howard: 'Nobody had informed me at one view I should see a palace, a town, a fortified city, temples on high places, woods worthy of being a metropolis of the Druids, the noblest lawn fenced by half the horizon and a mausoleum that would tempt one to be buried alive: in short, I have seen gigantic places before, but never a sublime one.'

Castle Howard, some fifteen miles from the city of York, still stands out among English country houses of the early years of the eighteenth century for its otherworldly quality. Like so many of the great country houses of the period, it speaks of the confidence of the age and yet looks back to the glories of Rome. It does so with a spirit of novelty that impressed contemporaries and still impresses today.

The house, certainly little short of a palace, stands on the crest of a hill and dominates the rolling landscape there. In its form and outline, bristling with urns, busts, and statuary, it symbolises the early-

eighteenth-century dream of the civilised life that was fostered in this generation by their reading of Classical literature and their travels in Italy and France. Even the imposing arrangement of the long and consciously dramatic approach, with its crenellated gates and walls and round towers, was probably intended to suggest Roman precedents as much as anything.

Vanbrugh brought a curious mixture of experience, wit and bravura to his role as architect to Castle Howard in 1699, when he was first commissioned by fellow Kit-Cat Club member, Charles Howard, 3rd Earl of Carlisle, to design a new country seat at Henderskelfe Castle in Yorkshire. Carlisle's family had owned the land since the sixteenth century.

Born in 1669, Carlisle had married at nineteen, and then made an extensive Grand Tour, as Viscount Morpeth. He returned to England in 1691 to live at Naworth Castle, near Carlisle. From 1695 he became involved in Whig politics, in the heady days following the Glorious Revolution. Although he seems to have run into conflicts with local political interests, William III apparently trusted his judgement. In 1701, he became a Privy Councillor, and from December that year he served as 1st Lord of the Treasury until May

1702 (William III having died in March 1702). He regained this post, for five months in 1715, under George I. Carlisle's commissioning of Castle Howard is therefore closely allied to his most active political period, intended, it is thought, to impress the new Dutch king, who was known to have an interest in architecture. He had also just acquired the estate from his grandmother, with a burnt-out castle at its centre. While this castle still afforded some degree of accommodation, a new house was needed – and what a house it was to be. As Hawksmoor observed of it in a letter of October 1734 to Lord Carlisle: 'It is the seat of one of the chief nobles of Britain, it is both a Castle and a Pallace conjoyn'd.'

Carlisle had first engaged William Talman for this work. In the 1690s, Talman, son of a country gentleman, was a key figure in the King's Works. In many ways, he was the leading country house architect, who had worked not only on Chatsworth for the 1st Duke of Devonshire, but also Dyrham Park in Gloucestershire for William Blathwayt, William III's Secretary of War. However, this talented architect was a difficult personality, who it seems no one could get on with, unlike Vanbrugh. He seriously displeased Carlisle and was dismissed. Carlisle's witty and capable drinking partner from the Kit-Cat Club, Captain Vanbrugh, was put in charge.

Whether confidence was placed in Vanbrugh because of his ability to engage Carlisle's imagination, or because of his sound good sense (which his kinsman, Lord Carmarthen, had described him possessing in battle) we cannot know. But there can be no doubt that he acted with remarkable speed, confidence and judicious self-instruction.

The east wing was constructed first in 1701–03, and offered temporary accommodation to the family until the main central block was completed by 1706. The principal apartments were mostly finished by 1712; the important interiors were mostly decorated by 1715. The plan and elevations (not quite as built) were published that year in the first volume of *Vitruvius Britannicus*, and an idealised bird's eye view appeared in the third volume in 1725. This key publication promoting the ambitious architecture of the age came to be seen as a polemic for the Palladian style, but Campbell could scarcely have overlooked the quality and scale of Vanbrugh's work at Castle Howard.

A detailed examination of the building accounts at Castle Howard is given in Charles Saumarez Smith's *The Building of Castle Howard* (1990). The western wing was completed to a different Palladian design by Sir Thomas Robinson, Carlisle's son-in-law and a gentleman amateur. That wing in turn remained unfinished until its interiors were fitted out by 1810–12. It is thought that the house (without Robinson's wing) cost around £38,000 to build, but, in 1738, with garden outworks and temples, Lord Carlisle calculated that he had spent nearly £78,000 altogether.

The bird's eye view published in the third volume of *Vitruvius Britannicus* (1725) shows both wings and service courts to east and

The south front of Castle Howard, seen from the south-west, showing the stately rhythm and grandeur of detail.

Above: *The impressive masonry dome, begun c.1703 and completed c.1706, was an unprecedented feature on an English country house.*

Left: *The central section of the south front, with the projecting central three bays under a richly decorated frieze of sea horses and shell-blowing tritons.*

west, although only those to the east were completed to Vanbrugh's design. It also shows three dramatic entrance gates that can be seen on a 1727 map, but are long since gone. The main entrance gate, on axis, was framed within four obelisks about which Carlisle and Vanbrugh, and no doubt Hawksmoor (who was obsessed with obelisks in his work), seem to have argued back and forth.

Vanbrugh's approach to the design is illustrated in a letter he wrote to the 4th Earl of Manchester on Christmas Day 1699. It also puts the astonishing ambition of Castle Howard in the context of other great houses of the day: 'I have been this Summer at my Ld Carlisle's, and Seen most of the great houses in the North, as Ld Nottings: Duke of Leeds Chattesworth &c. I stay'd at Chattesworth four or five days the Duke being there. I shew'd him all my Ld Carlisle's designs, which he said was quite another thing, than what he imagin'd from the Character yr Ldship gave him on't.'

Vanbrugh continued, with increasing confidence, stressing the Duke's positive reaction to his proposal: 'He absolutely approved the whole design, perticularly the low Wings, which he said wou'd have an admirable effect without doors as well as within, being adorn'd with those Ornaments of Pillasters and Urns, wch he never thought of, but concluded 'twas to be a plain low building like an orange house.' Certainly, the final version could never be thought plain.

The first house mentioned, 'Ld Nottings', was Burley on the Hill, Rutland, built for Daniel Finch, 4th Earl of Nottingham (a privy councillor who served as Secretary of State under William and Mary and then Anne); the second was Kiveton in Yorkshire for the 1st Duke of Leeds (Sir Thomas Osborne, Earl of Danby and Marquess of Carmarthen), the most prominent Tory to come out for William and Mary, who Vanbrugh had served under in the 1690s; and the third, Chatsworth in Derbyshire for the 1st Duke of Devonshire. The latter was a connection of Vanbrugh's mother by marriage, giving Vanbrugh a social introduction as well as a business contact.

Vanbrugh went on: 'There has been a great many Criticks consulted upon it since, and no objection being raised to't, the Stone is raising, and the Foundations will be laid in the Spring. The Modell is preparing in wood, wch when done, is to travel to Kensington where the King's thoughts upon't are to be had.'

This was a significant moment, and illustrates how Lord Carlisle used his ambitious plans for Castle Howard to catch the interest of the King. What is more, the Duke of Devonshire had just parted company with William Talman as his architect, even though Talman had certainly given him, in the rebuilt east and west ranges of Chatsworth, something of superlative national quality.

For Chatsworth is outstanding as the first great house in England in the Baroque spirit. It is also the first great house in which many of the finest talents who had previously worked on royal palaces were employed. But it was built in a surprising spirit of defiance for the Duke was in a period of self-imposed near-exile, such was the quickly

Castle Howard: in spirit both a palace and a castle; the lead sculptures are by Andries Carpentière. Photographed in 2001.

changing nature of the political world in the years following the Glorious Revolution.

This 1699 letter also underlines Vanbrugh's carefully considered ambition to create a building that competed with the leading contemporary English architects, and perhaps even to surpass them. This was an impressive ambition for a man newly turned to architecture as a profession, but as Pope later remarked he made no pretence of high scientific knowledge of the art of building. Yet he did have imagination, and he was also hugely conscious of Carlisle's interest in heraldry and genealogy. As Charles Saumarez Smith suggests: 'The buildings were intended to produce in the mind of the spectator an awareness of the lineage of the Howard family and of its place in history.'

The letter confirms that the designs were drawn up in 1699 and had been approved, and that site works and quarrying had begun. It also shows something of Vanbrugh's articulate way with words, the beguiling and reassuring way by which he sold his abilities to his clients. By words, he convinced them, as much as by action.

Architectural historians, such as Sir John Summerson, have compared the overall design at Castle Howard, with its great central block set between quadrant wings, to the unexecuted plan of 1693 by Wren for the Palace at Greenwich. He had envisaged a huge, domed central body, approached through a quadrant forecourt, later put away in favour of another, which preserved the vista to the Queen's House, designed by Inigo Jones.

Castle Howard also has some important echoes of famous French buildings of the second half of the seventeenth century, such as Louis Le Vau's Vaux-le-Vicomte (completed in 1661) with its central dome, and Jules Hardouin-Mansart's hugely admired Château de Marly, begun in 1679 for Louis XIV, notable for its use of the giant pilasters of the Corinthian Order. Talman's work at Chatsworth, and no doubt his proposals for Castle Howard, must have also played their role in shaping Vanbrugh's own designs.

Vanbrugh's principal departure from Talman's initial plan was the realignment of the house north/south, as opposed to Talman's east/west. This had practical advantages for both solar heating, and light, and undoubtedly improved the impact of the house as seen in the landscape. Vanbrugh's second even more ingenious innovation, not considered in his early plan, was the conversion of the originally

Right: The cymbal player by Andries Carpentière, photographed in 1926. Lead statuary played a key role in the Arcadian landscape created by Carlisle, Vanbrugh and Hawksmoor.

Below: Engraving of the overall plan of Castle Howard, published in Vitruvius Britannicus, Vol I, *1715.*

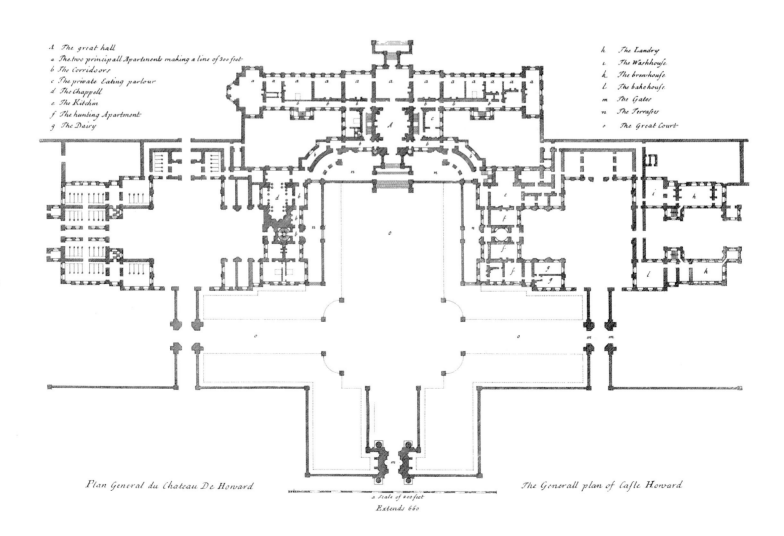

h The Landry
i The Washhouse
k The brewhouse
l The bakehouse
m The Gates
n The Terrasses
o The Great Court

Plan General du Château De Howard

a Scale of 200 feet
Extends 660

The Generall plan of Castle Howard

proposed central small cupola, so typical of late-seventeenth-century houses in England, into a fully fledged dome in the spirit of the recent work of Wren in London, and, perhaps more importantly, the highlights of contemporary Paris, such as the Collège des Quatre Nations.

The dramatic connection of the interior of the dome to the inner hall itself created at once one of the most memorable skylines of English architecture and an interior without parallel in English architecture at that time. In its splendid sculptural quality, the hall is perhaps more reminiscent of a crossing in a great church in Paris or Rome. It has been noted recently by architect Francis Terry that the source of the base detail of the great pilasters in the hall is taken from

Previous pages (left): *The extraordinary drama of the intersecting geometry of the Great Hall: one of the most sublime spaces in English architecture.*
(right): *The Great Hall has an unmistakably ceremonial flavour, as if Vanbrugh was reinventing the idea of aristocracy.*

Left: *An unusual view, taken in 1926, showing the disconcerting depth of the Great Hall, and the richness of carved detail. The gallery provides an additional viewpoint on the life of the house.*

Above: *The ceiling and pendentives were painted by Antonio Pellegrini. The pendentives represent the four elements: Earth, Fire, Air and Water.*

the pedestal details for the Corinthian and Composite Orders in the sixteenth-century treatise by Vignola: *Regole delle cinque ordini dell'architettura*.

The use of a dome on a private house was a novelty. It broke with the propriety that a dome was customarily reserved for a church (or the seat of a monarch as god's representative on earth). Palladio's Villa Rotonda, built for a Monsignor in charge of ceremonies at the Vatican, is an unusual exception.

The interior dome was painted with a scheme representing *The Fall of Phæton* by Giovanni Antonio Pellegrini, an Italian artist who seems to have come to England in around 1708. Phæton, the mortal son of Apollo, begged to drive the chariot of the sun, normally driven by his father, but, wish granted, he could not control it and he died in the attempt. The choice of subject is amusing when considered against Carlisle's political rise and fall. As Christopher Ridgway remarks in *Castle Howard* (1997): 'the 3rd Earl and Vanbrugh revelled in this dramatic tale of ambition and fall, which gently mocked their own aspirations.'

This splendid decoration was lost in a fire in 1940 when a number of interiors on the south front were burnt out, but the dome was

Previous pages: *The dome, showing* The Fall of Phæton, *rises over a clerestory. This photograph, taken in 1904, was one of those which provided key evidence for the reconstruction of the dome after a fire in 1940.*

Left: *Looking down to the Great Hall's* scaliogla *niche from the first-floor gallery and through to the west staircase behind.*

Right: *Looking up at the same view from the Great Hall, illustrating the multiple viewpoints contrived by Vanbrugh in the one stately room.*

rebuilt and its decoration repainted in the 1960s by the Canadian artist, Scott Medd. The painted pendentives under the dome represent the four elements: Earth, Fire, Air, and Water. These in turn rise from a heavily ornate entablature with richly carved composite capitals, which frame the room and draw the eye upwards. The dome sits on a drum, around which run a gallery and a series of windows allowing light into the hall.

Perhaps the most surprising and memorable element of Vanbrugh's design is the carefully contrived quality of interlocking spaces. This is achieved by the open character of the side walls, over the ornate stucco chimneypiece on one side and, on the other, over the *scagliola* alcove for statuary which faces it (both by the Italian stuccoists Bagutti and Plura). The openings form great arches above and allow views to and from the staircases, which rise behind.

The staircases arrive at the balcony-gallery, which allows the visitor to experience the theatrical nature of this remarkable room. Over the stairs themselves are painted scenes from the life of Apollo, god of music and poetry. Thus the view over the ornate chimneypiece allows a glimpse through the screen wall of *Apollo and the Muses*, look back and the story is that of *Apollo and Midas*.

Somehow, Vanbrugh had sufficient imagination and experience (or at least confidence) for all this. This derived in part from his ability to help realise Lord Carlisle's experiences on his Grand Tour, for Carlisle had travelled on the Continent in 1688–91, certainly visiting Padua and Vicenza and then Rome, and his notebooks record diligent attention to art and to Classical literature. He also demonstrated a continuing interest in Classical sources and Ancient Roman proto-types in his later works on the landscape at Castle Howard. Indeed, Carlisle is sometimes seen as a co-designer of Castle Howard.

Some of the development of Vanbrugh's original ideas must have been due to the expertise of his brilliant assistant, Nicholas Hawksmoor. For Vanbrugh, no doubt aware of his lack of real experience in managing a project of this kind, had appointed Hawksmoor as his assistant in 1700. He was probably the best-trained professional architect then available for such a project and was quickly set to work securing satisfactory estimates for the building.

Hawksmoor knew how to negotiate contracts, and was experienced in project management as he had been an assistant to Wren, Clerk of Works of Kensington Palace and at Greenwich Hospital, and chief draughtsman at St Paul's. Moreover, as demonstrated by Vaughan Hart's *Nicholas Hawksmoor: Rebuilding Ancient Wonders* (2002), even though Hawksmoor had never been abroad, he was widely read, and considered an authority not only on Classical and more contemporary architectural authors but also the relevant sciences. To quote his obituary: 'Nor was Architecture the only Science he was Master of … He was a very Skilful Mathematician, Geographer and Geometrician.'

Vanbrugh often referred to his and Mr Hawksmoor's opinion together, demonstrating that Hawksmoor's reputation also carried

The grand decorative stucco overmantel is thought to be the work of the Italian stuccoists Giovanni Bagutti and Signor Plura.

Above: *The collection of Antique sculptures was made by the 4th Earl of Carlisle.*

Left: *'Endless vistas at every turn'. The north corridor, photographed in 1926.*

Left: *The drama of the Great Hall is enhanced by the richness of the decorative detail, although the scale seems less daunting than suggested by photographs.*

Right: *The view from the west staircase. Classical statuary adds to the sense of theatre.*

considerable weight with his patrons. Hawksmoor, of more modest social origins than Vanbrugh, was inclined to be more deferential, although in later years when passed over for the job he coveted, he wrote of the Blenheim works: 'When the Building began, all of them put together, [the Builders] could not Stir an inch without me.'

Hawksmoor's command of the detail and management of the project is indicated in his communications with Lord Carlisle. For instance on 26 May 1701, Hawksmoor wrote to Carlisle: 'I find the work at Henderscelf to go on with vigour and grt industry altho there is not soe much done as I expected by this time ... I am come time enough to regulate some errours and difficultys the workmen were going into, and in generall the worke is firme and strongly performed.'

Hawksmoor's contribution to Castle Howard, and even more so to Blenheim (which he completed after Vanbrugh was dismissed) cannot be underestimated. Lord Carlisle respected and admired Hawksmoor who worked for him right up to his death in 1738; indeed Hawksmoor designed his famous rotunda mausoleum, thought to be the first free-standing mausoleum in the park of an English country house.

Hawksmoor clearly brought his skills as draughtsman and his understanding of the Classical Orders and the Vitruvian precepts of decorum in architecture to the style and detailing of Castle Howard, both of which Vanbrugh had the wit to allow to flourish in this design, and, more importantly, to learn from. Despite Hawksmoor's Classical knowledge, however, his use of the Corinthian Order on the south front and the Doric on the north was thought irregular by some. Hawksmoor observed defensively that the two sides could not be seen together at one time.

Castle Howard's plan was always palatial. It also developed in sophistication over the years of Vanbrugh's design and building. The *Vitruvius Britannicus* plan shows the proposed 'two principall Apartments making a line of 300 feet', either side of the saloon, approached via the great hall, itself flanked by staircases. The plan also illustrated the great long corridors aligned east/west, which linked the different parts of the house (one running across the north of the hall, leading to the wings, and one running across the south of the hall, leading to different parts of the main range).

Indeed, Vanbrugh has sometimes been credited with the introduction of the first corridor to an English country house – the Duchess of Marlborough was unfamiliar with the word, so in 1716 Vanbrugh explained that the corridor was a French invention: 'The word Corridor, Madam, is foreign, and signifies in plain English, no more than a passage ....' Although at Castle Howard the corridors run alongside the traditional *enfilade* openings between the rooms, they also allowed greater privacy.

The drama of this overall arrangement was caught well by Hussey and Tipping who wrote in 1928: 'the conception of vast extent given by the four galleries – of which one stretches forth from each corner of the hall, presenting almost endless vistas at every turn – has no

The garden hall looking through to the Great Hall. Taken in 1904, this photograph provides an important record of the room, which was destroyed by fire in 1940.

parallel in any English house.' Anthony Blunt also memorably said of Vanbrugh in his *Baroque and Rococo: Architecture and Decoration* (1978): 'he exploited the corridor, a rather new feature of house design for its perspective chiaroscuro.'

On the north front of Castle Howard, the originally plain elevation of one of the early designs, now held in the Victoria and Albert Museum, was made considerably more complex in its surface articulation and given the Doric Order. The elevation was also enlivened with sculptural figures in niches, representing the arts, banded rustication and a richly carved frieze. This gave an impressive overall degree of texture and detail, and was in part, at least, inspired by John Webb's treatment of the King Charles Building at Greenwich. The frieze of each pair of pilasters carries details of military emblems. The sculptures on the roof-line represent Socrates, Plato, Cicero and Seneca.

For the south or garden front, the consciously more elegant and splendid Corinthian was chosen, and a long sweep of round-headed sash windows, each crowned with an exaggerated keystone. Pevsner called this front 'eminently festive'. The designs evolved to include

the addition of a central pediment, with a richly carved coat of arms of Lord Carlisle.

The carving at Castle Howard was largely by Samuel Carpenter of York, who is recorded in 1705 as charging fifty shillings each for '27 Pilaster Capitalls of the Corinthian Order' for the south front of the main block. The Huguenot carver Mr Nesdos is thought to be the same Henri Nadauld who had worked at Chatsworth. In 1705, he was paid for work in the Grand Cabinet and in Lord Carlisle's apartment, as well as for the tritons, lions and trophies in the frieze of the entablature of the south front; and in 1710 he carved wood for the rooms on the south front.

Above: Looking east into the chapel at Castle Howard, fitted out in the mid-eighteenth century and lavishly decorated in the nineteenth century.

Right: The distinctive arches of the corridor in the east wing.

Overleaf (left): The gallery, which overlooks the Great Hall, and brings the viewer into intimate contact with the rich carving of the Corinthian capitals; photographed in 1926. (right): Looking back toward the Great Hall from the High Saloon, in 1904. The door surround details have been attributed to Giovanni Bagutti.

Chimneypieces were carved by William Harvey of York, while Bagutti and Plura, the two Italian stucco-workers, were responsible for the elegant composition of the chimneypiece in the main hall. The principal masons employed at Castle Howard were William Smith and John Ellsworth of York.

Carlisle presumably intended the interiors to equal the splendour of the architecture and, in 1706, paid John Vanderbank for tapestries for what was later described as the second state bedroom. These are thought to be the tapestries described by John Tracy Atkyns in his manuscript account of a 1732 visit to Castle Howard, quoted in Charles Saumarez Smith's *The Building of Castle Howard* (1990).

The description gives a good flavour of the sumptuous richness of the interiors in the lifetime of Lord Carlisle: 'a very beautiful mixture of colours, Chinese men & women in variety of postures all sorts of birds, beasts & fish.' Vanderbank also supplied hangings depicting the seasons, described by Atkyns as 'some of the most beautiful hangings that I ever saw done by Vanderbank.

Above: *The strikingly original and austere eastern service court has the impressive effect of extending the overall stately quality of the house with the same exaggerated height, suggestive of a fort.*

Right: *The entrance to the eastern court and the kitchen offices beyond.*

Below: *The stately east end of the house, with the family wing and eastern court behind; the west wing was completed to a different Palladian design.*

The imagination of the artist in tapestry is equal to the imagination of the poet.'

Coloured silks were supplied by the London Mercer, Remy George, including crimson damasks. Atkyns described the western state drawing room as 'a room hung with blew velvet, in it are 14 very large silver sconces, the whole furniture of the chimney of plate: the chimney of Italian marble after the model of Inigo Jones.' The richly layered state bed was described in the inventory after the death of the 4th Earl, as 'a 4 post Bedstead with Crimson Velvet furniture Gold laced and fringed with plumes of red & white ostrich feathers.'

Vanbrugh wanted the house to be considered practical as well as splendid. He was able to write in a letter of 29 October 1713 from Castle Howard to Edward Southwell, his client at Kings Weston: 'I am much pleased here (amongst other things) to find Lord Carlisle so thoroughly convinced of the Conveniencys of his new house, now he has had a years tryall of it.'

He continued: 'And I am the more pleas'd with it, because I have now a proof, that the Duchess of Marlborough must find the same conveniency in Blenheim, if ever She comes to try it (as I still believe she will in spite of all these black Clouds). For my Lord Carlisle was pretty much under the same Apprehensions with her, about long Passages, High Rooms &c. But he finds what I told him to be true. That those Passages would be so far from gathering & drawing wind as he feared, that a Candle wou'd not flare in them of this he has lately had the proof, by bitter stormy nights in which not one Candle wanted to be put into a Lanthorn, not even in the Hall, which is as high (tho not indeed so big) as that at Blenheim.'

And, as the draughts were contained, so the rooms were warm. 'He likewise finds, that all his Rooms, with moderate fires Are Ovens, And that this Great House, do's not require above One pound of wax, and two of Tallow Candles a Night to light it, more than his house at London did Nor in Short, is he at any expence more, whatsoever than he was in the Remnant of the Old house, but three housemaids and one Man, to keep the whole house and Offices in perfect cleanliness, which is done to such a degree, that the Kitchen, and all the Offices and Passages under the Principall floor are as dry as the Drawing Room.'

The continuing work on the landscape, which Carlisle pursued enthusiastically until his death in 1738, went on for the next three decades, to create that otherworldly vision of which Walpole wrote so enthusiastically, and to which we shall return in the chapter exploring the significance of Vanbrugh's thinking on landscape and garden design.

Houses, landscape, temples, were always seen as of a piece by Vanbrugh, as is clear from the descriptions in his letters. Our experience of the house today is tempered by the completion of the west wing in 1753–59 to a different design by Carlisle's son-in-law,

The belvedere designed by Vanbrugh for Lord Carlisle, now known as the Temple of the Four Winds, a homage to Palladio's Villa Capra, La Rotonda.

Sir Thomas Robinson, which has the effect of concealing much of the drama of the main house on the approach.

In 26 August 1721, Vanbrugh wrote to Brigadier Watkins: 'My Lord Carlisle going on with his Works as usual; by which the Seat is wonderfully improv'd this last Year. Two Years more, tho' they won't compleat all the Building, will so Beautify the Outworks, of Gardens, Park, &c, That I think no Place I ever Saw, will dispute with it, for a Delightfull Dwelling in generall, let the Criticks fish out what particular faults they please to the Architecture.'

It would be wrong to leave off an account of the glorious story of Castle Howard without mentioning Vanbrugh's charming homage to Palladio: the belvedere, now known as the Temple of the Four Winds. It was begun only in 1725 and was completed in 1738, twelve years after Vanbrugh's death. Vanbrugh and Hawksmoor had clearly discussed possible variations, and one of Hawksmoor's surviving sketches is inscribed as, 'The Belvidera – After ye Antique. Vid Herodotus/Pliny, and M: Varo'. The corners of the temple are marked: 'Books, Chimny, Drains, and a bot wine', which must refer to the Classical precedents of Pliny the Younger's Villa Laurentium, near Ostia, and the eating parlour of the Roman scholar, Marcus Terentius Varro.

Hawksmoor observed of Vanbrugh's design, in a letter to Lord Carlisle: 'What Sr John proposes is very well, and founded upon ye Rules of ye Ancients. I mean upon Strong Reason and good Fancy, Joyn'd with experience and tryalls, so that we are assured of ye good effect of it, and thats what we mean by following ye Antients, if we contrive to invent otherways, we doe but dress things in Masquerade, which only pleases the Idle part of mankind for a Short Time.'

Kerry Downes has observed of this temple: 'In the clear North Yorkshire air it has an unexpectedly Mediterranean aspect, entirely and marvellously in harmony with the Virgilian feeling of its land-scape setting. In his final tribute to Palladio Vanbrugh came closer to the spirit of the great Italian's Roman gravity, which he had never seen, than did many an architect who had made the Grand Tour.'

It was Vanbrugh's final temple. It was mentioned in a letter of 11 February 1724: 'My Lord Morpeth about a month ago. View'd all the Designs I had sent, declar'd his thoughts utterly against anything but an Italian Building in that Place, and entirely approv'd the first Design.' A week later, Vanbrugh wrote: 'And for the Porticos them-selves nothing can be more agreeable than the Seats under them.' Not least, perhaps, for the opportunity – he imagined hopefully – to sit and look back towards the glorious house he had helped to create with such brilliant panache.

The magnificent mausoleum designed for Lord Carlisle by Hawksmoor, inspired by the Roman tomb of Metella.

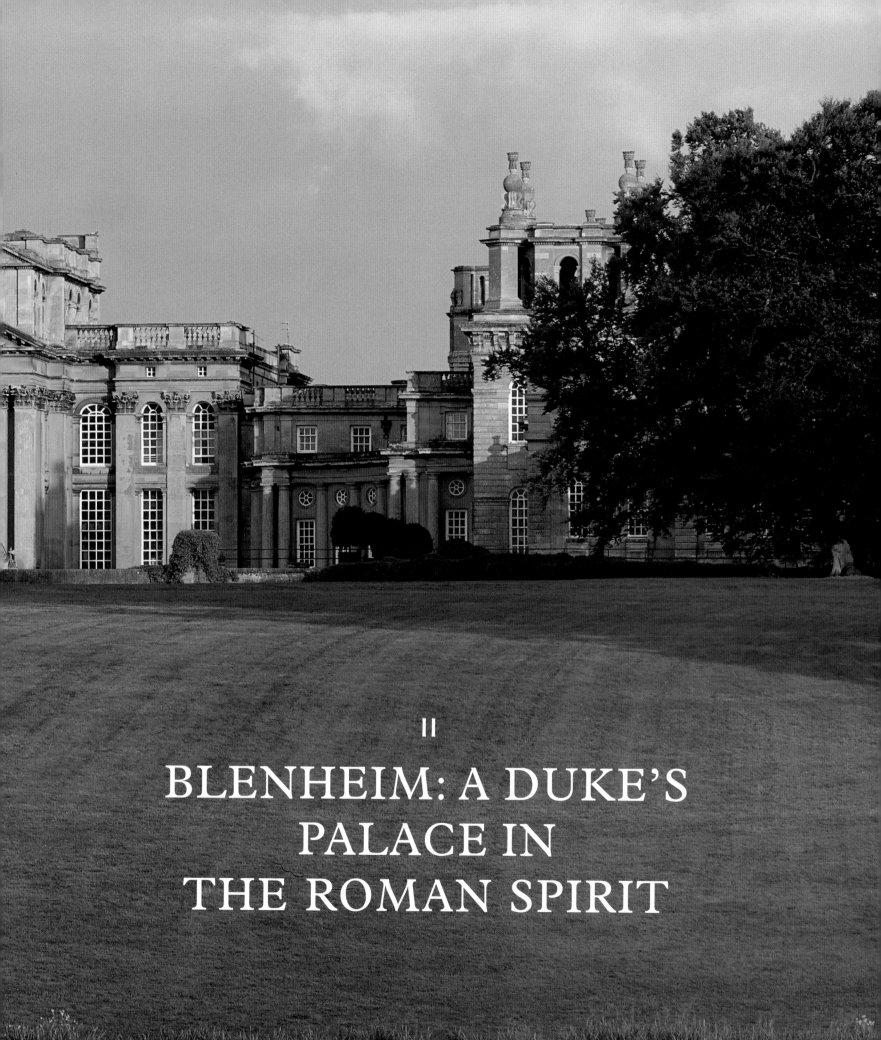

II
BLENHEIM: A DUKE'S PALACE IN THE ROMAN SPIRIT

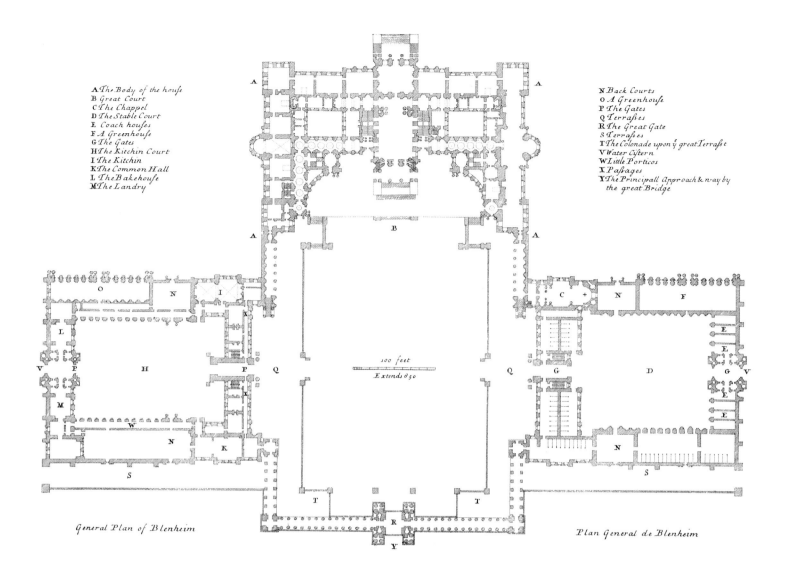

100 feet
Extends 850

General Plan of Blenheim   Plan General de Blenheim

Uvedale Price in his *Essay on the Picturesque* (1794) praised the sight of Blenheim by evening light: 'Whoever catches that view towards the close of evening, when the sun strikes the golden balls and pours his beams through the open parts, gilding every rich and brilliant ornament, will think he sees some enchanted palace.'

Vanbrugh's bravura in his designs for Castle Howard led directly to the more demanding commission to design Blenheim, on which work began in 1705. It was a project on a great scale, which grew in ambition during the building process, and despite the famous problems that beset the project, it was mostly completed by the early 1720s and became a national triumph, in visual impact as well as in the Classical sense of a celebration of victory.

Blenheim was an immense, complex and drawn-out building project and only an outline of the story can be given here. The extensive building accounts, much of which are now in the British

Library, formed the basis of David Green's great work *Blenheim Palace* (1951) and further explored in the work of Kerry Downes.

The grant of Woodstock Manor was a gift from Queen Anne and a grateful nation after the Duke of Marlborough's great victory at Blindheim. The English and allied armies, alongside troops commanded by Eugene of Savoy, had defeated those of France and Bavaria on 13 August 1704, the decisive if not concluding victory in the War of the Spanish Succession. This was a war that had begun over the right to the throne of Spain, but also became one of checking the power of France (a grandson of Louis XIV had inherited the throne of Spain as Philip V).

The nation's hero, John Churchill (born in 1650) began life as a fairly impoverished page in the Stuart court and rose through charm and soldierly qualities. He was encouraged first by James, Duke of York (later James II), and fought in the Battle of Sedgmoor, during the Monmouth rebellion. Churchill later supported the invitation to William III and Mary to take the throne and was made Earl of Marlborough. In 1690, he served in Ireland, although he fell out of favour after being suspected of intrigue with the exiled court. Marlborough was by nature a Tory, but by default became the hero of the Whigs.

Previous pages: *Blenheim Palace from the south: emphatically a palace in scale and grandeur, it was originally called Blenheim Castle.*

Above: *The overall plan published in* Vitruvius Britannicus, *Vol I, 1715; the stable court was not fully completed.*

Left: *The east gate designed by Vanbrugh, and built in 1708; note how the heavy tapered pilasters appear to rest on cannonballs.*

At the accession of Anne he was made Captain-General of the army, and became a duke in December 1702. This was partly due to his talents as a soldier and administrator, but also to his wife's connections with the Queen. Marlborough had married Sarah Jennings, the daughter of a Hertfordshire gentleman, in 1678. She was a childhood friend of Queen Anne, and in 1702 was made Groom of the Stole, Keeper of the Privy Purse, and Mistress of the Robes. The Marlboroughs thus became one of the most powerful private couples in British history. Their eldest daughter married the son of the Lord Treasurer, Lord Godolphin, a close ally of the Churchills from his early days and a leading Whig.

There is no doubting Marlborough's brilliance as a soldier. He ranks with Wellington as one of the greatest military commanders in British history. Furthermore, Marlborough's decisive victory at Blindheim (Blenheim) put England centre-stage as a power broker in Europe; the nation was appropriately grateful. There seems to have been general agreement that as well as the gift of the old royal manor of Woodstock, the civil list would fund the building of a house, but when a crisis came five years later, no document could be found.

One biographer, William Coxe, in *Memoirs of John, Duke of Marlborough* (3 vols, 1818–19), recorded what was no doubt the family view: 'Not satisfied with that the nation alone should testify its gratitude, the Queen accompanied the grant with an order to the Board of Works to erect, at the royal expense, a splendid palace which in memory of the victory was to be called the Castle of Blenheim. A model was immediately constructed for the approbation of the Queen and the work was begun without delay, under the direction of Mr (afterwards Sir John) Vanbrugh.'

Originally, the house was called Blenheim Castle. It became known as Blenheim Palace in the nineteenth century, not least because the building is so fundamentally a palace in all respects. Peter Wentworth in 1713 thought, with some justice, that it looked like 'a great college with a church in the middle'. Abel Evans wrote skittishly in one contemporary satirical verse:

> Thanks sir', cried I, 'tis very fine
> But where d'ye sleep or where d'ye dine?
> I find, by all you have been telling,
> that tis a house but not a dwelling.

This breathtaking building, every bit as aesthetically overwhelming as Uvedale Price described it, is still the seat of the dukes of Marlborough. In the early 1700s, it was probably the single most ambitious project in Britain for a private family. Naturally, its design reflected its status as a national memorial as well as a residence of a great man. As Vanbrugh wrote in 1709: 'Tho' ordered to be a Dwelling house for the Duke of Marlborough and his posterity [it was] at the same time by all the world esteemed and looked on as a publick edifice, raised for a Monument of the Queen's glory.'

Awesome and unforgettable grandeur: the north front of Blenheim, with the projecting temple front entrance, and the raised clerestory over the Great Hall.

In another letter of 30 September 1710 he wrote of Queen Anne's intentions, as he understood them: 'When the Queen had declared she would build a House in Woodstock parke for the Duke of Marlborough, and that she Mean't it in Memory of the Great Services he had done her and the Nation, I found it the Opinion of all people & of all partys I convers'd with, that altho the Building was to be calculat'd for, and Adapted to, a private Habitation, Yet it ought at y same time, to be consider'd as both a Royall and national Monument, and care taken in the Design, and the Execution, that it might have y Qualitys proper to such a Monument, Vizt Beauty Magnificence and Duration.'

One 1720 legal brief gives Vanbrugh's own account of his first conversation with the Duke about Blenheim: 'About xmas 1704 he meeting casually with the Duke in the playhouse in Drury Lane the Duke told him he designed to build a house in Woodstock park and expressed his intention of not exceeding a certain sum, which to best of deponents remembrance was 40,000£.' How remarkable to consider the glamorous national hero of battle approaching the glamorous hero of the theatre on his own territory – the meeting

preceded by some months the official confirmation of the grant.

By February 1705, when Vanbrugh first visited the site, the Duke had already inspected the model for Castle Howard and decided that he was the man for the job. His demands were straightforwardly ambitious: he wanted something suitable for a leading citizen, something of the same kind as Castle Howard, but with the addition of a picture gallery. A Treasury warrant, from the Lord Treasurer, Lord Godolphin, of 9 June 1705 appointed Vanbrugh as the Duke's surveyor and agent. Vanbrugh then appointed the invaluable Hawksmoor as his deputy. By 1706, there were 1,000 people working on the site.

The building project was immense and Vanbrugh's and Hawksmoor's powers of administration were inevitably put to the test. There were other key players, of course, such as the comptrollers at

Above: *The entrance to the kitchen court, on the east side of the house, crowned by a clock tower.*

Right: *One of a pair of British lions squeezing a French cockerel, carved by Grinling Gibbons for the kitchen court gateway.*

Above: *The ceiling of the Great Hall at Blenheim, painted by Thornhill, appears almost to float over a great clerestory of windows.*

Left: *The great arch of the Hall, reminiscent of a proscenium arch in a theatre.*

Blenheim, William Boulter and Henry Joynes, and the masons, Edward Strong, father and son, who had worked with Wren, supported by John Townesend and Bartholomew Peisley of Oxford. The plasterers were Robert Wetherill and Isaac Mansfield; Hopson and Smallwell were joiners; Banks and Barton, carpenters. The elaborate formal gardens were designed by Henry Wise, gardener to Queen Anne.

The ambition of the project was reflected in the final cost. Marlborough had wanted to spend around £40,000. Asked to provide an estimate, Wren suggested around £90,000 – £100,000 (without the side wings). The final cost was close to £300,000, of which the Treasury eventually paid a large proportion, after long delays. (This was over six times what Castle Howard had cost and around £25 million in modern money).

While we know that it was proposed that Blenheim should, in part at least, follow the model of Castle Howard, there was always to be a degree of greater magnificence. Indeed, the level of grandeur suggests more than a nod to Versailles, the spectacular palace of Louis XIV, whom Marlborough had defeated in battle. There are certainly similarities to Castle Howard in the overall plan: an imposing double-height hall, flanked by staircases, with a saloon behind at the centre of a long garden front, and Vanbrugh's characteristically dramatic long corridors.

But Blenheim's plan is noticeably deeper and thus more deliberately palatial in layout, initially to accommodate the picture gallery proposed by Marlborough, which became the long gallery or library on the west front. There was no portico or clerestory in the initial

Right: The saloon: one of the most magnificent rooms in England, finished after Vanbrugh's resignation in 1716.

Below: The painted architecture and fictional crowds add a sense of state and drama to the saloon; the scheme was inspired by Le Brun's L'Escalier des Ambassadeurs at Versailles.

Left: *Detail of the decoration of the saloon, painted by Louis Laguerre.*

Right: *The saloon door-cases bear the double-headed eagle of the Holy Roman Empire, of which Marlborough had been made a prince.*

proposal, but there was also considerable evolution of the design in the early years of building. Something like the finished versions of Blenheim's elevations and plans appeared in the first volume of *Vitruvius Britannicus* in 1715.

By 1707, the overall design of the entrance front was felt to be too low and the decision taken to heighten the whole building. At the same time this required Vanbrugh to dispense with the masculine and martial associations of the Doric Order, which were replaced by the more splendid and more expensive Corinthian. This required pulling down a considerable amount of the walls, already built, of the south front.

Another alteration, that undoubtedly transformed the impact of the principal elevations was the creation of the clerestory, which brought daylight light flooding down into the interior of the Great Hall, so making the huge ceiling appear almost suspended in mid-air. It gave the room the theatrical quality of a vast public space, as much as the entrance to a private house.

In 1707, Vanbrugh wrote to the Duke: 'in the first entrance of the House; where by bringing the break forwarder, the Hall is enlarg'd, and from a round is brought to an Ovall, figure, a Portico added and Yet the Room much better lighted than before. And the top of it rises above the rest of the building in the middle of the Four Great Pavilions. I hope your Grace will like this alteration for it adds wonderfully (I think) to the Beauty, regularity and Magnificence of the Building.' Things were going well in 1708 and Vanbrugh wrote, on 14 September: 'I dare Answer for it, that all shall be coverd in Two Summers more.'

He also remarked confidently: 'And as to Expense it will Appear at last, That there has been such husbandry in the design (which is the Chief Concern) as well as in the Execution, That the Whole will by all People be judg'd to have Cost full twice as much as will be paid for't.' However, that same year Vanbrugh began work on his elaborate bridge over the River Glyme, which earned the particular displeasure of the Duchess, but remains a monument to his scenographic skills as designer (to which Capability Brown responded later in the eighteenth century with the creation of the great lake).

Even so, the final form of the portico was not apparently decided in April 1708 when the Duke wrote to the Duchess: 'I am advised by everybody to have the Portico, so that I have written to Vanbrook to have it.' As a result of this decision, the central composition at Blenheim becomes one of unforgettable originality and power. The quadrant sections conceal smaller rooms and staircases to the east and west of the main entrance. They also add to the imposing presence of the main front, and draw the eye to the two arcades, which push forward into the great court.

One of the most memorable features of Blenheim, which emerged at this stage of the design, was the set of four elaborate open towers, added to the roof-line. Their complex Classical form was devised by

The Long Library at Blenheim, finished by Hawksmoor, and originally conceived by Vanbrugh as the picture gallery for the Duke of Marlborough's collection.

Hawksmoor, based on a demolished Roman temple at Bordeaux, as recorded in Perrault's 1673 edition of Vitruvius's books of architecture.

They are also echoed in the pair of chimney groups at each end of the great house, effectively adding another two turrets (making the roofscape as lively as an Elizabethan power house, such as Burghley or Longleat). The larger turrets were apparently tried out in full-scale model versions in 1707, just to judge the visual effect. The four pinnacles of each tower originally had an inverted French fleur de lys surmounted by the Duke's coronet, carved by Grinling Gibbons for £20 apiece. Gibbons and his workshop were responsible for most of the external carving.

The south front is less complex in its parts and therefore, perhaps surprisingly, more sedately grand in feel. Its fluted Corinthian columns and pilasters add richness and character to the central block, which projects forward. Tall ground-floor arched windows, which light the state apartments, lead the eye away to the corner towers, with their elaborate turrets on top.

Like Castle Howard, Blenheim was planned to be hugely extended to either side, with additional courtyards to east and west, although only the kitchen court was finished and the stable court was left incomplete. As well as having practical benefits they were undoubtedly intended to add to the stately and commanding fortress quality of the house, which was always, from the very outset, to be covered with martial trophies.

In fact, the images of war are everywhere you look. Here, a trophy of arms and armour in the ancient manner; there, cannon balls in stone; over the north entrance front stands Pallas Athene, between two figures of chained captives, while over the south front peers a bust of Louis XIV, captured at the siege of Tournai in 1709. Among the best details are the highly amusing sculptures of the British lion clutching the French cockerels, on either side of Vanbrugh's gigantic gateways to the kitchen and stable courts.

The interior is equally heroic. As you pass inside, you encounter the magnificent Great Hall – surely at 67ft high, one of the most memorable rooms in England. Its high ceiling painted by Sir James Thornhill in 1716 depicts *The Glorification of the Duke of Marlborough*, with the Duke kneeling before Britannia, gesturing to a plan of the battle.

Across from the entrance, and framed between two huge Corinthian attached columns, stands the great arch, rather in the spirit of a great proscenium arch in a grand theatre, springing from the entablature above paired Corinthian columns. Behind the arch runs the first-floor balcony, as at Castle Howard, suggestive of a platform to watch a performance below.

Even one of Vanbrugh's harsher critics, Thomas Hearne, conceded in 1717 that 'the Hall is noble'. On each side the massive walls are

The First State Room (as photographed in 1909), with one of the tapestries depicting the campaigns of Marlborough. This one shows the despatch from the battlefield of Blenheim with the news of victory. The Louix XIV-style plasterwork was added in the 1890s.

pierced by two storeys of arches, behind which, on one side, a great staircase rises. The arches create a powerful sense of weight, while at the same time drawing the eye out of the great central space. At both the front of the room and at the back, two great corridors intersect, made up with domed compartments, which have been compared to the side aisles of St Paul's Cathedral.

Beyond the hall at the centre of the state apartments on the south front, lies the great high-ceilinged saloon. It is decorated with *trompe l'œil* architecture of columns and a series of painted trophies of arms, and oval windows painted in relief with trumpeters leaning through. From the colonnade painted in relief, figures peer down – a reference to Marlborough's rank as a prince of the Holy Roman Empire, for as a prince he would have been expected to dine in public. The artist was Louis Laguerre (ironically a godson of Louis XIV). On the white marble doorcases are two-headed eagles, another reference to Marlborough's princely rank; the doorcase to the west was carved by Grinling Gibbons.

The richly appointed state apartments, which subsequently received later layers of interior decoration, are still hung with a series of

---

Left: *The elegant Bow Window Room contrived by Vanbrugh as a sitting room for the Duchess of Marlborough.*

Below (left): *The carved marble chimneypiece in the Duchess's bedroom, designed by Vanbrugh and carved by Grinling Gibbons.*

(right): *The carved marble chimneypiece in the Bow Window Room.*

tapestries by Judocovus De Vos, woven in Brussels by Lambert De Hondt especially for the house. They depict the great battles in which Marlborough fought and underline the flavour of the house as a celebration of a hero's career.

The west front contains one vast room: the gallery-library, 180 feet in length, with a central bow window. While on the east front is another bow, which serves the Duchess's own boudoir at the centre of what are still the private apartments. These novel bow windows (which also form an unusual composition with the groups of chimneys above) have been compared to the brilliantly accomplished bow windows at Burghley, still considered to be masterpieces of late Elizabethan design. Between the two bows runs the main corridor which intersects the Great Hall.

In 1708, Vanbrugh had been full of spirit and confidence, writing on 27 July to Lord Manchester of the 'Vast Progress there', adding, 'I met John Coniers there on thursday last, with Severall Virtuoso's with him; He made mighty fine Speeches Upon the Building, And took it for graunted No Subjects house in Europe woud Approach it; which will be true, if the Duke of Shrewsbury judges right in Saying there is not in Italy so fine a House as Chattesworth, for this of Blenheim is beyond all Comparison more Magnificent than that.'

As the project progressed Vanbrugh, very much the appointment and friend of the Duke, found his relationship with the Duchess of Marlborough increasingly difficult. She was clearly an extremely forceful character, who proved herself to be a 'good hater'. To give

her her due, she seems not to have been behind a grand project from the start, saying: 'I never liked any building so much for the show and vanity, as for its usefulness and convenience.'

She also wrote of Vanbrugh: 'for at the beginning of the work I never had spoake to him, but as soon as I knew him and saw the madness of the whole Design I opposed it all that was possible for me to do ....' She told her granddaughter that 'painters, poets, and builders have very high flights and must be kept down.' She also dismissed poor Thornhill for charging as much for sky as for figures.

With the Duke away fighting, in 1709 the Duchess defiantly commissioned a town house from Wren – a no doubt calculated rebuke to Vanbrugh. The Duke wrote to Sarah from Rotterdam on 9 June: 'I do wish you all happiness and speed with your building at London but beg that it may not hinder you from pressing forward the building of Blenheim.' In September, he wrote: 'I am so persuaded

that this campaign will bring us a good peace that I beg of you to do all you can that the house at Woodstock may be carried up as much as possible that I may have a prospect of living in it.'

The Duchess's debacle with Vanbrugh is now so famous it is easy forget the successful years of their relationship and their mutual respect, before things were brought to a head by the new Tory-dominated administration under Lord Harley, which slowed the pace of Treasury payments almost to nil. The Duchess naturally wanted to see the Duke resident in his great house, but with Marlborough closely associated with the Whig faction, after Lord Harley became Lord Treasurer the generosity of the state to the Marlboroughs was openly questioned.

This uncertainty over Treasury payments caused a serious crisis in 1710 and in the summer of that year Blenheim's principal mason, Edward Strong, laid off most of his workforce. In 1711, the Duchess, for so long one of Queen Anne's favourites, had her own catastrophic

The west front of the house, showing the bold effect of the corner towers and the architectural impact of the three-storey bow.

fall from grace, falling out bitterly with the Queen, and the Duke was then also dismissed from all his posts, and accused by his political enemies of trying to prolong the war for his own benefit. In 1712, the Duke and Duchess went into informal exile. In 1713, Vanbrugh also lost his post as Comptroller of The Queen's Works.

With the accession of George I in 1714, the Marlboroughs were immediately restored to court favour (and Vanbrugh to the comptrollership, with a knighthood to boot) and things looked brighter for the completion of Blenheim. Vanbrugh had been of the party that received King George and was knighted at Greenwich – an event recorded spitefully by Thomas Hearne who wrote that 'the first knight that King George made is one Vanbrugh a silly fellow, who is the architect at Woodstock.'

In July 1716, Vanbrugh was directing works and wrote to the Duchess with a curious reference to the old manor at Woodstock (which he had tried to persuade her to keep), in relation to the choice of style for the side courts: 'I have set the Oxford Masons upon the office in the Kitchen Court and do promise your Grace I will have the homely simplicity of the Antient Manor in my constant thoughts for a guide in what remains to be done, in all the inferior Buildings.' But it was difficult to resume the Blenheim project with equanimity, particularly after the Duke suffered his first stroke in 1716.

There is a wealth of detailed correspondence about Blenheim in Vanbrugh's edited letters and accounts, analysed in Kerry Downes's two books on Vanbrugh. A good example of the tensions between the Duchess and Vanbrugh is that of 8 July 1709, when Vanbrugh recorded a discussion with the Duke about 'a little kind of Salon' (which the Duchess objected to) at the end of the greenhouses: 'that on the Stable side, having a Very beautiful Situation ... looking

directly down the Valley and the River) may perhaps be thought proper for a distinct retir'd room of Pleasure, furnished with only some of the best Greens, mixd with pictures, Busts, Statues, Books, and other things of ornament and entertainment.'

But Vanbrugh's vision was not shared by the Duchess. He defended it to the Duke, arguing that the 'Tytian hangings' could be hung there and it would double as a library: 'The Books dispos'd in Presses made handsome like Cabinets, And plac'd Regularly along with the Chairs, tables And Couches ... it seems clearly to me the most Valluable Room in the Whole Building.' The Duchess won and noted on the letter: 'The second greenhouse, or a detached gallery I thank God I prevented being built; nothing, I think can be more mad than the proposal, nor a falser description of the prospect.'

By November 1716, Vanbrugh had resigned from Blenheim – his fights with the Duchess too much to bear. On resigning his commission he wrote: 'You have your end Madam, for I will never trouble you more. Unless the Duke of Marlborough recovers so far, to shelter me from such intolerable Treatment.' He wrote too of her accusations of mismanagement: 'These Papers, Madam, are so full of Far-fetched, Labour'd Accusations, Mistaken Facts, Wrong Inferences, Groundless Jealousies, and strain'd Constructions, that I

shoud put a very great affront upon your understanding.' Later, he described her as 'that B.B.B.B. Old B. the Duchess of Marlbh.' Vanbrugh could be a good hater too.

In 1721, the Duchess tried unsuccessfully to sue Vanbrugh and others involved in the building. Initially, after Vanbrugh's departure, the work was continued by her cabinetmaker, James Moore. But after 1722 Hawksmoor took charge. He saw it through to its near completion by 1725, and ruefully compared himself in a letter to: 'a Loving Nurse that almost thinks her child her own.'

The completion of the building was no mean feat, and perhaps no one but Hawksmoor, already responsible for much of the working detail of the project, could have achieved this in the way that he did. The private apartments in the east wing were sufficiently finished to receive the Duke and his family in 1719, and a grand entertainment was given in which the Duke's grandchildren acted out Dryden's *All for Love*, stage managed by Steele, with a specially written prologue by Bishop Hoadly.

Above: *The diversity of detail in the roof-line illustrates the provocative genius of Vanbrugh and Hawksmoor at Blenheim; the north-east tower is in the centre of this view.*
Right: *A note of leonine surprise: a carved lion's mask.*

Marlborough died in 1722, leaving Duchess Sarah to a long and bitter widowhood during which, however, she erected for her beloved husband one of the finest funerary monuments in Britain in the chapel at Blenheim. It was designed by William Kent and carved by Rysbrack. Rysbrack also carved the figure of Queen Anne that stands in the library and the bust of the 1st Duke in the same room.

But we should not let the complexity of the building history detract from the fact that Blenheim is a magnificent piece of architecture. The drama of the roof-line and composition of Blenheim, as much as the vigour and authority of the architectural detail, makes this one of the most notable buildings of the age.

William Mavor, in *A New Description of Blenheim* (1789), wrote that Vanbrugh 'rendered this structure characteristic and expressive of its destination. Its massy, its spacious portals, and its lofty towers, recall the ideas of defence and security; with these we naturally associate the hero for whom it was erected, and thus find it emblamatic of his talents and pursuits.'

Blenheim has a memorable outline. It has prompted generations of scholars to note the possible inspiration of prodigy houses, such as Wollaton in Nottinghamshire (designed in the 1580s by Robert Smythson), or even fourteenth-century castles like Herstmonceaux in Sussex, with its central gatehouse and corner towers.

Vanbrugh certainly displayed a particular consciousness of the qualities of historic architecture that he encountered on his travels, remodelling Lumley Castle and persuading Lord Newcastle to reoccupy Nottingham Castle. Giles Worsley has suggested that at Blenheim in particular, given the nature of the project, Vanbrugh was trying to develop something of a new British 'national style', drawing on Classical sources, and the great buildings of British history. The kingdom of Great Britain was formally created by the Act of Union in 1707.

Some critics have been extremely harsh about Blenheim, as in September 1717, when Alexander Pope wrote: 'I never saw so great a thing with so much littleness in it. I think the architect built it entirely in compliance to the taste of its owners, for it is the most inhospitable thing imaginable, and the most selfish; it has like their own hearts, no rooms for strangers … In a word, the whole is a most expensive absurdity, and the Duke of Shrewsbury gave a true character of it, when he said, it was a great Quarry of Stones above Ground.' Horace Walpole waspishly recorded visiting the house in 1736: 'nothing but a cross housekeeper and an impertinent porter, except a few pictures, a quarry of stone that looked at a distance like a great house.'

But, placing witty put-downs on one side, it is difficult not to admire the ambition and sense of theatre of this building, the joint masterpiece of the two most influential British Baroque architects. Among twentieth-century architectural critics, Anthony Blunt wrote

in *Baroque and Rococo: Architecture and Decoration* (1978): 'Its imagery is that of Versailles and its language is one of complex rhythms and textures, large scale and rich three dimensional modelling both in its main masses and in Hawksmoor's details; in all this, and in such eccentricities as the broken and stepped-back pediment over the entrance, it sustains comparison in the international phase of Baroque, with major works of Fischer von Erlach and Juvarra.'

Vanbrugh and Hawksmoor created something original and unforgettable. Sir John Summerson wrote of Blenheim in *Architecture in Britain 1530–1830* (1953): 'those separated fragments which are the last things one remembers of Blenheim and which leave a hint of doom, like the crag of an antique ruin.' The ambition of the house remains breathtaking, its presence massive and monumental. As Laurence Whistler wrote in 1954: 'It was at Blenheim that the two architects discovered the epic style together; and afterwards they practised it separately, according to a difference in temperament.'

Pitifully, although largely completed by Hawksmoor in 1723–25, Vanbrugh was never given the chance to go round Blenheim in the company of his great collaborator. He tried to visit, but as he wrote to his friend, Jacob Tonson, on 12 August 1725, in a scene not a little reminiscent of the confused comical scenes of his own plays, he failed: 'We Stay'd Two Nights in Woodstock, My Lord and the Ladys, having a mind to View Blenheim in every part with leisure. But for my own Share, There was an order to the Servants, under her Graces own hand, not to let me enter any where.' Nor did the Duchess leave it at that.

Vanbrugh continued mournfully: 'And lest that should not mortify me enough, She having some how learn'd, that my Wife was of the Company sent an Express the Night before we came there with orders, if she came with the Castle Howard Ladys the Servants shou'd not Suffer her to see either House, gardens, or even to enter the Park, which was obey'd accordingly, and She was forc'd to Sit all day and keep me Company at the Inn.' How one would like to know more of his thoughts and observations as he peeked at his great creation by looking over the fence from the Woodstock Rectory.

Previous pages: *Detail from the Rysbrack tomb depicting the 1st Duke of Marlborough as victorious commander.*

Left: *The elegant marble tomb in Blenheim's chapel dedicated to John, 1st Duke of Marlborough, designed by William Kent and carved by Rysbrack in 1733.*

III

VANBRUGH'S ENCHANTED
CASTLES

When in Vanbrugh's play *The Relapse*, Young Tom Fashion and his servant Lory approach the feudal seat of Sir Tunbelly Clumsey, the servant exclaims: 'I'gad, sir, this will prove some inchanted castle: we shall have the giant come out by and by with his clubs, and beat our brains out.' It is impossible to look at the country houses designed by Vanbrugh and not sense his fascination with the English castle, which led to his version of the castle style – his 'embattled manner', as Laurence Whistler called it in *The Imagination of Vanbrugh and His Fellow Artists* (1954).

Several architectural historians, including Kerry Downes and Giles Worsley, have explored the intriguing notion that Vanbrugh was interested in the formation of a national style for the age. Whether or not this philosophical and practical endeavour was on Vanbrugh's mind when creating a lasting national memorial at Blenheim, the dramatic outline of great English castles of the fourteenth century may well have been an influence.

Vanbrugh may also have been touched by the intervening interpretations of the chivalric castle outline, such as early-seventeenth-century Bolsover Castle in Derbyshire, which overlooked the Great North Road and was owned by his friend Thomas Pelham-Holles, the Earl of Clare (later 1st Duke of Newcastle). The continuing significance of a castle as a symbol of noble status, as well as of private retreat, would have appealed to Vanbrugh's sense of decorum.

Vanbrugh's early years as a professional soldier (he resigned in 1698 as a captain of marines) exposed him to contemporary and

Previous pages: The east front of Kimbolton Castle, Cambridgeshire. Vanbrugh re-ordered the house from 1707–10 for the 4th Earl, later 1st Duke, of Manchester. The portico is now thought to have been designed by Thomas Archer.

Above: The south front of Kimbolton Castle, Cambridgeshire, with the stables designed by Robert Adam beyond.

Right: The east front of this stately castellated house. Vanbrugh had evoked the 'castle style' for it in keeping with its long fortified history. It was thought by him to have a 'Noble and Masculine shew'.

traditional theory of fortification and may have fuelled his interest in fortified buildings. This may be more relevant to the bastions and outworks he often designed around gardens, such as at Castle Howard and Seaton Delaval, as Robert Williams discussed in his essay on fortified gardens in *Sir John Vanbrugh and Landscape Architecture in Baroque England 1690–1730.*

Vanbrugh's visual and literary imagination were possibly also influenced by his years in prison at the Château de Vincennes and in the Bastille in Paris – a theme explored in detail by Frank McCormick in *Sir John Vanbrugh: the Playwright as Architect* (1991). Moreover, Vanbrugh's childhood was spent in the shadow of the surviving medieval city walls of Chester, which then still encircled the whole city and would have added to the associations of strength and history in his mind. His family moved there by 1667, when he was a very young child, possibly to avoid the plague. The castle and city walls withstood two sieges by Parliamentary forces before capitulation, but

contemporary illustrations show that crenellated walls, towers and gates still enclosed the city, which was dominated by the cathedral and the tower of St Michael's Church.

Vanbrugh did make at least one specific reference to the towers of the city walls during his architectural career and that quite late on. In November 1724, he wrote to Lord Carlisle referring to the admirable example of the Chester walls. To the idea of a spire, he said: 'a Cap is all that those sort of Towers shou'd have, and I have seen one upon a round Tower on the walls at Chester, that I thought did extreamly well.'

But even more revealing are the remarks he made about his work in 1707–10 at Kimbolton Castle, near Huntingdon, for his kinsman the 4th Earl of Manchester, who was then serving as the King's Envoy to Venice. One of Vanbrugh's earliest architectural commissions after Castle Howard and Blenheim, Kimbolton was Lord Manchester's already multi-layered family seat, a complex and much rebuilt courtyard house.

The original fortified manor house, dating back to around 1200, had been rebuilt around the courtyard by Ann, Duchess of Buckingham in the mid-fifteenth century, and further remodelled by

Above: The saloon at Kimbolton Castle, designed by Vanbrugh, is the central room of the south front.

Left: The great staircase designed by Henry Bell, and painted in 1708 by Antonio Pellegrini.

Sir Richard Wingfield in the sixteenth century. In the late seventeenth century, it was partly redesigned by the talented gentleman amateur, Henry Bell of King's Lynn.

Kimbolton Castle was also famously the house to which Katherine of Aragon retired after her divorce in 1534. It was acquired by Sir Henry Montagu in 1615, who became 1st Earl of Manchester in 1621. (The 2nd Earl, a Parliamentary commander, was later the Speaker who received Charles II on his return from exile). Vanbrugh helped to bring the whole complex together in a new spirit of symmetry, but surprisingly chose to do it in a fortified style.

Vanbrugh's patron, Charles Montagu, who became the 4th Earl of Manchester at his father's death in 1683 and was created 1st Duke in 1719, ranks as one of Vanbrugh's highly educated and well-travelled patrons. He was, with Vanbrugh himself, a noted patron of the arts bringing Italian opera to London and the two corresponded about engaging Italian musicians to come to the city. He had studied at

Trinity College, Cambridge, and travelled on the Continent in the mid-1680s, during which he had an audience with the Prince of Orange, later William III.

Like others in the select circle of Vanbrugh's patrons, the 4th Earl was a man of action, who had experience of military command. He had raised a troop of cavalry and joined William when he landed in England and later fought alongside him at the Battle of the Boyne. In 1691, he married Dodington Greville, daughter of the 4th Baron Brooke. In 1697–98, while Envoy to Venice, he tried to negotiate the release of imprisoned English seamen. In 1699–1701, he was appointed Ambassador to Paris and in 1707–08 he returned to Venice to try and negotiate the Republic's support for the Grand Alliance. It was during this later time abroad that Vanbrugh was called in to help with the family seat.

Part of the south front of the house had collapsed and the rest had then been dismantled for safety. The Countess, Vanbrugh wrote to

The south front of Kimbolton Castle, Huntingdonshire, the first of the elevations to be remodelled by Vanbrugh; photographed in 2005.

the Earl, 'did me the honour (when she saw it must do so) to, ask my Advice in carrying it up Again', as the local carpenter, William Coleman, first called in to effect the repair was finding the job of bringing the design together a challenge.

Among other things, Vanbrugh observed: 'he had not brought the Door of the House into the Middle of the Front', and to achieve this elegant symmetry Vanbrugh extended the front. He felt strongly that there should be a way out of 'this Front into the Garden' and was therefore resolved on an unusual, but he felt amusing, disposition of the rooms: 'I thought there cou'd nothing in reason be Objected to being Surpris'd with a large Noble Room of Parade between the Drawing Room and Bedchamber; especially since it falls so right to the Garden.' The Countess persuaded him not to make his saloon as

large as he first planned, so as to preserve Henry Bell's staircase (painted by Pellegrini by 1709) and not to lose any bedrooms.

More interestingly, despite this formal symmetry, Vanbrugh used what we might call the 'castle style', with a crown of crenellation over regularly placed sash windows, and smooth ashlar walls. Vanbrugh described his choice with confidence, even with poetry, supported by a judicious appeal to economy. On 18 July 1707, he wrote: 'As to the Outside, I thought twas absolutely best, to give it Something of the Castle Air, tho' at the Same time to make it regular. And by this means too, all the Old Stone is Serviceable again; which to have had new wou'd have run to a very great Expence; This method was practic'd at Windsor in King Charles's time, And has been universally Approv'd.'

As if conscious that Lord Manchester would be surrounded by well-versed Italian connoisseurs of architecture (and perhaps English ones as well) who might be amazed to find the Earl putting up an old-fashioned castle, and not a more Classically-inspired villa in the Italian spirit, he continued: 'So I hope your Ldship won't be discourag'd, if any Italians you may Shew it to, shou'd find fault that 'tis not Roman, for to have have built a Front with Pillasters, and what the Orders require cou'd never have been born with the Rest of the Castle: I'm sure this will make a very Noble and Masculine Shew; and is of as Warrantable a kind of building as Any.'

In another letter of 9 September 1707, Vanbrugh pronounced himself happy with the design and to have won over the local man as well: 'I lik'd mighty well what was done, And Coleman Own'd he begun to discover a Gusto in it, that he had no Notion of before. I shall be much deceiv'd if People don't See a Manly Beauty in it when tis up, that they did not conceive cou'd be produced out of such rough Materialls; But tis certainly the Figure and Proportions that make the most pleasing Fabrick, And not the delicacy of the Ornaments: A proof wch I am in great hopes to Shew yr Ldship at Kimbolton.'

On 17 August 1708, he wrote how the new front 'looks extreamly well from the farther end of the Canall.' He continued: 'I hope yr Ldship will find the Appartment within, worthy of the good furniture you have provided for it. The Velvet is to be downe on friday, and great expectation there is of it.' In the same letter he mentioned the Earl's engagement of the Venetian painter Giovanni Antonio Pellegrini: 'If the painter yr Ldship brings over be a good one, he may find work enough; but the New Room at Kimbolton can't be ready for him this Winter. So I Suppose you'll Set him Upon the Hall.'

He also persuaded Lord Manchester to let him reface the rest of the house, which was done in stone in 1710. Vanbrugh's elegant saloon was finished soon after. The Doric portico on the east front, added by 1715, is now thought to have been designed by Thomas Archer. A plan also survives for the steps that lead to it by the Florentine architect, Alessandro Galilei.

Vanbrugh's next major private commission (excepting Castle Howard and Blenheim on which he was still busy) was Kings Weston, near Bristol, on which he worked from 1710 to 1719 – another demonstration of a 'Noble and Masculine Shew' although the castle element is lighter and even more unexpected. It certainly holds a special place in Vanbrugh's work, perhaps at a scale and in a setting that suited his temperament. As Tipping and Hussey observed in 1927, the actual building is one of the smallest that he worked on, 'but has all his individuality.'

The building is broadly Classical and Italianate in character, with bold Corinthian pilasters on the south front under a triangular pediment, but entirely un-Classical in feel is the unforgettable grouping of the chimney-stacks into three-sided sided prominence with a distinctive, almost castellated silhouette. On 23 October 1713, Vanbrugh wrote of making 'tryall of the heights etc., with boards' to judge the effect.

Gate piers at Kings Weston, near Bristol, where Vanbrugh worked from 1710.

In its dramatic position above the Bristol Channel, Kings Weston ranks as one of Vanbrugh's 'enchanted castles'. It might be seen, as Hussey suggested, as a castle from a painting by Claude – particularly when viewed from out to sea, perhaps the very route that the patron of the house, Sir Edward Southwell, would take between his responsibilities in Ireland and England.

Southwell was a civil servant of considerable education who had studied at Oxford and at Lincoln's Inn and been elected to the Royal Society in 1692. Kerry Downes notes that Southwell kept a journal on his visit to Holland in 1696, which shows his interest and understanding of architecture. In the first volume of *Vitruvius Britannicus* (1715), Colen Campbell referred to Southwell as 'the Angaranno of our age', a reference to the famous patron of Palladio (to whom Palladio dedicated the first two volumes of *I Quattro Libri*, and for whom he began, but did not complete, the Villa Angaranno).

His father was a cultivated lawyer and President of the Royal Society, who had spent a considerable time touring in Italy in 1660. He was entertained by the Grand Duke of Tuscany and his brother in Florence, and in turn entertained him on his Irish estates at Kinsale in 1669. Sir Edward's son, also Edward, went on an extensive tour of Italy, spending three months in Rome in 1725–26, recording thoughts in his journal on ancient civilisations.

In 1703, Southwell married Lady Elizabeth Cromwell, daughter of the 4th Earl of Ardglass. He was appointed chief secretary to the 2nd Duke of Ormond, then Lord Lieutenant for Ireland. Lord Egmont wrote of Southwell: 'No man led a more pleasant life. He was beloved by all his acquaintance for his cheering, obliging temper.' He attended William of Orange in 1688, and travelled with him on his Irish campaign. He later sat as an English Member of Parliament after 1713.

He was considered a moderate Tory – moderate enough to employ Vanbrugh, a man so identified with the Whig cause. The rebuilding of Kings Weston coincided with his first attempt to become a Member of Parliament in the election of 1710, after the death of Lady Elizabeth in 1709, and before his second marriage to Anne Blathwayt, daughter of the builder of Dyrham Park in Gloucestershire.

Letters between Vanbrugh and Southwell in 1713 suggest the patron's close attention to the detail of the project as shown in one of 23 October: 'As to the objections you mention, I can only say I cannot think as they do, tho' it may be I am wrong. As to the door being too little, if an alteration be thought necessary I can show you how to do it; but of these particulars of it is better to talk than to write.' The master mason was one George Townsend of Oxford, who also worked at Blenheim.

Approached by a flight of steps, Vanbrugh's house (altered by architect Robert Mylne later in the eighteenth century) was a dashing conception: an entrance, through a not over-large door, brought the visitor into a double-height entrance hall, it appears it was originally

The pedimented south front of Kings Weston, Gloucestershire, designed for Sir Edward Southwell, MP.

open on two levels to the double-height staircase beyond. The staircase, which survives, is a particular *tour de force*, as it rises without visible supports across the space of the hall, looking as much a technical exercise as anything else. A plan for some of the parquetry, on the stairs, survives and is dated 1719.

As in other of Vanbrugh's designs, a balcony-cum-gallery once ran across the staircase hall, east/west, connecting the first-floor rooms, and would originally have allowed views down into each public room. Around the staircase hall are a series of tall, curved niches with *trompe l'œil* urns and Classical statues.

The plan of the house is effectively U-shaped, and thought to follow something of the earlier house (as can be seen in an engraving by Kip). The important ground-floor rooms were placed along the west and east fronts (while the two halls occupied the central portion of the house): the western rooms looking out across the channel, and the eastern ones looking up towards a typically Italian loggia, with lively rusticated detail, approached by a steep path.

Another pedimented temple slightly to the north-west of the house,

and dated to around 1718, is composed around a Serliana (or Venetian window) opening, with a lunette under the pediment, reflecting the arrangement of the south front. But Vanbrugh also designed various outbuildings and stables at Kings Weston, not least a handsome brewhouse, distinctly in the castle style, with pronounced corbelling. A number of designs, which survive in the Bristol Record Office, refer to landscape works, including a great court with an entrance topped with a pyramid.

Perhaps Vanbrugh's most famous use of the castle style, however, was for his own little house built in 1718–1719 on top of Maze Hill. overlooking Greenwich Hospital, of which his brother had been secretary to the Hospital committee since 1695. Vanbrugh himself was knighted there by George I in 1714. He became Surveyor to

Above: The hall of Kings Weston, adapted in the 1760s by Robert Mylne, was originally designed to have a first-floor arcade connecting with the staircase hall behind.

Right (above): Vanbrugh's brilliant 'flying' staircase seen from the first-floor landing. (below): The staircase seen from ground level; the blind arches are painted in trompe l'œil to suggest statuary and urns.

Greenwich Hospital, succeeding Wren, in 1716. His first country retreat at Chargate, near Esher, in Surrey was also castellated, but lost its crenellation after 1715 when the house was extended for the Earl of Clare, later 1st Duke of Newcastle.

Vanbrugh took a 99-year lease from Sir Michael Biddulph for a 'Field & other Grounds' at Greenwich. Vanbrugh Castle was constructed, in brown London stock brick, by the bricklayer Richard Billinghurst, and largely complete by December 1719. The castle was originally compact and rectangular in plan with three storeys over a basement. Three narrow four-storey towers create the appearance of the castle to the south front side; the two corner towers are crenellated, the central round stair tower topped with a cap.

The north front, which overlooks Greenwich Hospital, was originally much narrower with a central three-storey bow window, giving the appearance of a tower. When first built, at a distance, it would have been seemed more upright, even alert, standing as it still does on the sudden falling away of the hill. Vanbrugh Castle was also originally constructed on a strictly symmetrical plan, which only came to be asymmetrical with later accretions. There was a good reason for these.

For in 1718, at the advanced age of fifty-two, Vanbrugh married Henrietta Maria Yarburgh, daughter of Colonel James Yarburgh (a former aide de camp to the Duke of Marlborough) of Heslington Hall in Yorkshire. They quickly began a young family and had two sons – Charles, named after his godfather Lord Carlisle, and John who died young – and a daughter who died at birth. Charles lived to adulthood, was a commissioned army officer and died of his wounds at the Battle of Fontenoy in his twenties.

Vanbrugh's family required substantial additions to what may well have been considered something of a bachelor pad; he had clearly surprised some of his friends by his marriage to the young Henrietta Maria, herself a second cousin of the Duchess of Newcastle, wife of his patron. Vanbrugh's letters hint at his forthcoming marriage only in this charming aside to Lord Newcastle: 'tis so bloody Cold, I have almost a mind to Marry to keep myself warm.'

The rooms of the original Vanbrugh Castle are not at all large, and the carefully composed vaulted corridor and circular staircases are positively small, but they are comfortable. The plan is very neat, perhaps Palladian in inspiration. The house would probably have been furnished simply, but hospitably, perhaps in the spirit of the speech of Sir Tunbelly Clumsey in *The Relapse*: 'Get a Scotch-coal fire in the great parlour; set all the Turkey-work-chairs in their places; get the great brass candle-sticks out and be sure to stick the sockets full of laurel.'

A sense of family was clearly important to Vanbrugh and he built a number of other notably unusual houses for his siblings on his small estate here. One, known as Mince Pie House, was the home of his brother, Captain Charles Vanbrugh, and was like Vanbrugh's castle

The east front of Kings Weston, Gloucestershire, with its surprisingly austere elevation and highly original chimney-stack arrangement.

in spirit, a rectangular banded block with engaged round towers at each end.

Vanbrugh designed another single-storey house, more Italianate in inspiration, but with a central square tower, which was nicknamed The Nunnery, and thought to have been lived in by Vanbrugh's unmarried sisters, Victoria and Robina. Both houses were surrounded by walls, giving each a further dash of castle style. There were certainly medieval style gateways and other garden structures.

These included a tower built, he claimed, for the amusement of his son. He wrote in 1722 to Lord Carlisle, his two-year-old son Charles's godfather, that the boy 'is much pleas'd with a House I am building him in the Field at Green[wic]h: it being a Tower of White Bricks, only one Room and a Closet on a floor.'

These outlying structures were demolished in the early 1900s, but William Stukeley sketched all the Vanbrugh estate buildings in 1722 and some early-twentieth-century photographs of them appear in Tipping's *In English Homes, Late Stuart 1649–1714*, Vol IV (1928).

Above: *The remarkable arcaded chimneys of Kings Weston give an oddly castellated feeling to the silhouette.*

Top: *The arcaded loggia sited at the top of a walk, allowing a view to the house and beyond to the Bristol Channel*

Left: *The finely detailed Serliana opening of the loggia at Kings Weston.*

Stukeley's 1722 sketch shows the main castle building wrapped around with crenellated walls and towers and a gatehouse that create an almost fairy-tale composition. The castle was approached through an arched gateway, between two-storey square towers, which were also demolished as was another gateway to the estate in 1902.

As well as its fairy-castle flavour, it is interesting to note that his house would have been a near neighbour to Wren's Royal Observatory, which lies just west of it, the residence of the Astronomer Royal, a symbol of the world of ideas and scientific advancement. What is more, the principal rooms, and the roof, had an exceptionally clear view not only of Greenwich Hospital but the city crowned with Wren's dome for St Paul's. Access to the roof to see this view was through the main stair turret. Vanbrugh Castle must have felt almost 'in the air'.

Vanbrugh was known to muse about the fictional castle-ness of his castle. In a charming aside in a letter to Lord Newcastle, who had visited his house when he was absent in 1723 in Yorkshire, he toyed with the idea of the nature of his castle-home. 'I hear your Grace was pleas'd to Storm my Castle yesterday, I hope next time you'll be so Gallant to lt me know of your Design, which If I do, I'll endeavour to give you a Warmer Reception.'

It is impossible to consider Vanbrugh's attitude to the castle style without paying some attention to his work at Lumley Castle in Co. Durham. It was built for his friend, Richard Lumley, who became 2nd Earl of Scarborough in 1721; his father, the 1st Earl had been a favourite of Charles II in his youth, and commanded a regiment during the Monmouth Rebellion. Later, he was a colonel in the Life Guards and subsequently became one of the leading courtiers who

Above: Vanbrugh's own home, Vanbrugh Castle in Greenwich. The ingenious use of arches and vaulted passage extend the sense of space and architectural dignity in a relatively modest space.

Left: *The house was originally contained between the two narrow square towers, but was extended to the right after he married in 1718 and had children.*

invited William of Orange to claim the English throne and fought at the Battle of the Boyne. The 2nd Earl also later became a lieutenant-general in the army.

Of Lumley Castle, Vanbrugh wrote in August 1721: 'Lumley Castle is a Noble thing; and well deserves the Favours Lord Lumley designs to bestow upon it; In order to which, I stay'd there near a Week to form a General Design for the whole, Which consists, in altering the House both for State, Beauty and Convenience, And making the Courts, Gardens and Offices Suitable to it; All which I believe may be done, for a Sum, that can never ly very heavy upon the Family. If I had had good weather in this Expedition, I shou'd have been well enough diverted in it; there being many more Valluable and Agreeable things and Places to be Seen, than in the Tame Sneaking South of England.'

Works were also mentioned in a letter early the next year. On 24 April 1722, Vanbrugh wrote to Lord Carlisle that 'My Ld

Scarborough tells me he certainly go's to Lumley Castle the end of May, and has desir'd me to propose some things for him in order to begin his Works there. What I shall be able to do, I don't yet know; but my desires are strongly Northward, especially to Castle How[ar]d.'

In essence, Vanbrugh preserved the overall outline of the castle, especially the four corner towers with their late fourteenth-century diagonal buttresses and crenellation – the original licence to crenellate was given to Sir Ralph Lumley in 1389. Vanbrugh also respected all the heraldic and historical decoration introduced by John, Lord Lumley, in the late sixteenth century, including the sequence of full-length portraits of significant martial monarchs he later appears to have imitated at Grimsthorpe Castle.

That Lord Lumley had been inordinately proud of his pedigree. When James I visited on his journey south in 1603, he was shown round by the Bishop of Durham, whose long lecture on the Lumley pedigree going back and back further in history, drew the famous retort: 'oh, mon, gang na further. I maun digest the knowledge I ha' this day gained, for I didna' ken Adam's 'ither name was Lumley.'

The south side of the castle was remodelled by Vanbrugh to give serviceable grand living rooms on the principal floor, and a new

Above: *The west front of fourteenth-century Lumley Castle, Co. Durham: Vanbrugh remodelled the central range, introducing the tall sash windows and roundels above.*

Left: *The Romantic silhouette of Lumley Castle, where Vanbrugh worked for the 2nd Earl of Scarborough, photographed in 1910.*

corridor and another broad staircase, added in a compartment set back within the courtyard. The new corridor was divided into three parts, with handsomely detailed Serliana screens, in the manner of Venetian window openings, with Roman Doric columns. This was a motif which Vanbrugh often employed in many of his later works, and probably derived from Palladio. He also altered the basement vault of the south-west tower.

The Great Hall in the west side was also modernised with the introduction of a series of sash windows, and round windows above, replacing earlier Gothic windows, and a new doorway. The great Classically-inspired 1570s chimneypiece was retained and other earlier sculptural elements preserved. Sash windows were introduced all over the castle.

As Hussey and Tipping observed in 1927: 'To such confirmed medievalists as the late Sir St John Hope, Vanbrugh's alterations were "blemishes". We however see in them a capable adjustment of old forms to new requirements, of a Gothic structure to the call of a Whig magnate for a "palazzo" disposition', but Vanbrugh, 'alone of the professionals of his day' achieved this 'without destroying the dramatic outline and picturesque grouping of Ralph Lumley's fourteenth century house.'

To borrow Vanbrugh's own phrase used regarding Kimbolton, his work at Lumley Castle certainly made 'a Noble and Masculine Shew' – a phrase that describes so well the architecture of Vanbrugh in all its manifestations and particularly those of a 'Castle Air'.

Lumley Castle's Great Hall as remodelled by Vanbrugh.

IV

VANBRUGH'S LAST GREAT HOUSES

The twentieth-century Romantic painter John Piper described a visit to Seaton Delaval Hall, near Newcastle, in *Buildings and Prospects* (1948): 'Vanbrugh the man of the theatre was at least as operative here as Vanbrugh the architect. In this last work he created a rich stage which, when the footlights were turned down and the smart audiences gone, would adapt itself to any kind of bad acting and if necessary would carry on with the play itself.' How well he caught the dramatic impression of a first encounter of this remarkable house.

Seaton Delaval was one of the last three major country houses designed by Vanbrugh. As with Eastbury in Dorset and Grimsthorpe in Lincolnshire, it was also largely unfinished at his own death in 1726. They were all works of bold, original conception, and each special to its own context. At the same time, they each displayed the same key themes of status and civilisation. The principal elevations in

Previous pages: *Grimsthorpe Castle, Lincolnshire, seen from the west; the towers to the left are part of Vanbrugh's remodelling begun in 1723.*

Above: *The north front of Seaton Delaval Hall, near Newcastle, a new house designed by Vanbrugh in 1721 for Admiral Delaval. It is Classical in inspiration, yet almost castellar in outline.*

Left: *The stable wing of the forecourt to Seaton Delaval Hall, Northumberland.*

the Classical style were enhanced by towers, wings and deep fore-courts put together in unconventional fashion and conveying a stately palatial quality.

They were also commissions largely independent of his association with Nicholas Hawksmoor. However, it is probably futile to try and make this distinction, so fully would Vanbrugh have imbibed the knowledge and architectural approach of his friend and assistant. The plans of all three houses were consistent with his knowledge of Palladio, and all three were published in the third volume of *Vitruvius Britannicus* (1725).

Eastbury, described as 'New design for a person of quality in Dorsetshire', was designed for George Dodington (d.1720), a wealthy financier, MP and supporter of William III. He was also a cousin of Viscount Cobham at Stowe. The house was completed by Roger Morris, and considered to rival Blenheim in scale, but it was demol-ished later in the eighteenth century, with only a side gate and stable block surviving to be adapted to a house. These remains still hint at the gargantuan scale of the original house – the elevations, garden plan by Bridgeman and vast temple, with a portico the same height as the Pantheon, were all illustrated in *Vitruvius Britannicus*.

Seaton Delaval Hall, begun in 1721 and completed in 1728, is one of Vanbrugh's most complete masterpieces. It stands in a dramatic elevated position, some ten miles from Newcastle, overlooking the sea. As Tipping and Hussey observed in 1927, Vanbrugh's inspirational sources were 'on the one hand, an abstract feeling for related masses; on the other the fairy castles of Claude and Gaspard Poussin, the tragedies of Dryden.' The main block, damaged by fire, has not been inhabited since the 1820s, which adds to the Romantic flavour enjoyed by Piper and many visitors since.

It was built for Admiral George Delaval (born in 1660) who had

accumulated wealth as the result of a successful naval career, and was a distinguished diplomat and Envoy to the Emperor of Morocco, with whom he settled a treaty for the redemption of British prisoners of war. In 1710–13 he became Envoy Extraordinary to the King of Portugal; in 1715, he was elected as Whig MP for West Looe in Cornwall. He bought the Seaton Delaval estate in 1717 from a distant cousin, Sir John Delaval, the 3rd and last Baronet, thus rescuing the family estates from disintegration, and sustaining an ancient line settled there since the twelfth century.

Although clearly well travelled and literate in later life, not much is known of the Admiral's education. A tantalising memoir, quoted in J. Robinson's *The Delaval Papers* (1880) but since lost, mentioned a tour taken in 1709, partly in the company of Henry Newton, the British Envoy to the Grand Duke of Tuscany, which included visits to Genoa, Florence and Rome. Robinson certainly believed this memoir belonged to George Delaval, and this, together with his period in Morocco and Lisbon, would probably make him one of the more

Previous pages: *The concentrated architectural drama of the arcade at Seaton Delaval Hall, Northumberland, which runs along the stable wing, with a glimpse of the stirring centrepiece of the north front.*

Left: *Writhing lead figures of David and Goliath (probably by Bandinelli) add appropriate drama at Seaton Delaval Hall.*

Below: *The artist John Piper captured the extraordinary mood of Seaton Delaval in his 1941 painting.*

visually sophisticated of Vanbrugh's interesting circle of patrons. Newton incidentally was the agent who arranged for sculptures to be sent to Blenheim.

On 18 February 1717, the Admiral wrote to his brother: 'I should tell you that Sir J. Vanbrugh built Castle Howard, and it is from thence I hope to carry him.' And a few days later: 'I intend to persuade Sir John Vanbrugh to see Seaton if possible & give me a plan of the house, or to alter the old one, which he is most excellent at; and if he cannot come, he'll recommend a man at York who understands these matters. So something may be done degrees & be the entertainment of our old age, or as long as we can live. I am much out of order with the Scurvy.'

The two men obviously enjoyed a rapport, which Vanbrugh seems to have established easily with military men. Vanbrugh wrote on 26 August 1721 to Brigadier Watkins from York: 'the Admiral is very Gallant in his operations not being dispos'd to starve the Design at all. So that he is like to have, a very fine Dwelling for himself, now, and his Nephew &c hereafter.' Delaval was unmarried and childless and his heir was a nephew, Captain Francis Blake Delaval.

The Admiral may well have seen Castle Howard on his journeys south. His initial intention was probably for a remodelling, but it seems he was persuaded by Vanbrugh to begin anew. The York

mason, William Etty, supervised the works, according to a letter from Sir Thomas Robinson (5 June 1721) noting that Etty had 'gone to Admirall De Lavalls to lay ye foundation of his house.' The plan and elevations published in the third volume of *Vitruvius Britannicus* (1725), are dated 1721.

This main north-facing entrance front has a novel arrangement of three columns at each corner, which suggests a fragment of an ancient temple. The Doric frieze is picked out with carvings that include subjects such as a warrior's head, a griffin and an eagle. The upright towers at each side of the building both contain well-lit oval, open well, stone staircases.

The whole front is framed by an immensely deep open courtyard (180ft long and 152ft broad) with two pavilion wings connected to the house by short curved corridors, while an elegant, if squat, arcade runs the whole length of each wing – the east containing the stables, completed later in the eighteenth century, the west containing the kitchens and servants' quarters.

Right: *The extraordinary and highly original centrepiece of the north front of Seaton Delaval Hall, Northumberland, framed between a group of three Doric columns which enclose the corners.*

Below: *The compact Palladian-inspired plan of Seaton Delaval, with its dramatically long forecourt, as it appeared in* Vitruvius Britannicus, *Vol III, 1725.*

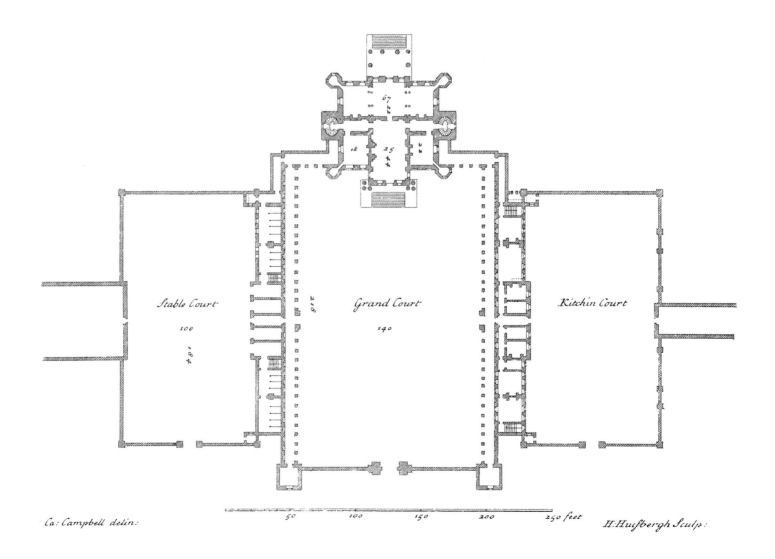

Ca: Campbell delin: 50   100   150   200   250 feet   H. Hulsbergh Sculp:

The wings are deliberately low and link effectively to the basement of the central block, and thus serve both to emphasise the stately compactness of the rusticated entrance elevation with its Serlio-derived centrepiece, and the bold giant order and banded Doric columns which frame it. The rippling effect of the banded rustication and the colour in the stone adds to the feeling of strength.

It is an extraordinary and original composition on which the eye of the observer can hardly rest for a moment before being drawn in another direction to new details: the exaggerated keystone, or the novel treatment of the banded columns. The high pediment (in front of what was clearly an attic floor devoted to the views in all directions, including out to sea) is filled with the handsomely carved Delaval arms.

The south front, facing the Delavals' extensive landholdings, has a four-columned (tetrastyle) portico in the Ionic Order, and is, as Hussey and Tipping observed in 1927, 'as smiling as the north was grim'. The Serliana, or Venetian, windows also appear on the east and west side.

But Seaton also illustrates Vanbrugh's ability to use different elements in a convincing and original whole. This memorable building, its architecture so carefully composed, faces north. Though on first glance one sees it as a Classical villa between symmetrically disposed long wings, its composition and particularly the effect of the stair turrets at either side and the half-octagonal bays have long inspired architectural historians to read references to medieval, Tudor and Jacobean ones, such as Wollaton or Bolsover Castle. These eye-catching buildings could hardly be avoided by anyone taking the Great North Road.

Previous pages (left): *Looking up through one of the elegant open staircases at Seaton Delaval Hall, Northumberland.*
(right): *The main hall, damaged by fire in 1822.*

Above: *The south front, with the east and west stair towers.*

Right: *The house seen from the south-west, the stately Ionic portico supports a balcony.*

The main block is surprisingly compact, at just 75ft by 75ft. The plan of the house, as published in the third volume of *Vitruvius Britannicus* (1725), is amazingly simple and probably derived from Palladian prototypes. Sarah Lang and Giles Worsley both compared it to Palladio's plan for Villa Pogliano.

The principal floor is raised up over a basement level, in the manner of a *piano nobile*, and the double-height entrance hall, approached by a flight of steps, has a smaller panelled chamber on either side. A central corridor runs on axis, east/west, connecting to the two stair turrets. The north-east room beside the hall was fitted out in bolection-moulded mahogany panelling, mentioned in a letter of 1724. The other chamber was described in eighteenth-century inventories as the tapestry room.

The stairs and the corridors were eminently practical, making good use of space and enough survives to show this. The first-floor corridor ran as a gallery in the great entrance hall (rather in the same way Vanbrugh contrived at Castle Howard and Blenheim). The whole of the south front was devoted to a large saloon – 75 ft long by 30 ft wide and divided by screens of columns into three parts – which in turn opens out on to the deep projecting portico.

William Hutchinson described the saloon in *A View of Northumberland* (1778): 'In this room there are eight majestic fluted Corinthian columns of the most beautiful stone, and the same number of pilasters, which divide it into three spaces. The ceiling was executed by the famous Italian artist, Vercelli, and is exquisitely modelled, and admirably coloured.' Vercelli was probably the Italian stuccador, Francesco Vassalli, who worked at Castle Howard in the 1720s. He was probably also responsible for the figures of the liberal arts that still stand in the blind arcades in the hall.

The roofs of both porticoes would have provided impressive viewing platforms both towards the sea and the land, and the Admiral is known to have started considerable plantations of trees. A surviving letter from his agent Mewburne, 10 December 1720, listed 200 elms just planted and 800 limes still to plant.

The garden to the south was enclosed at some distance by a ha-ha, which had prominent circular bastions at the corners. As early as 1717, the Admiral had written to his brother imagining his retirement: 'making a garden and planting forest trees, for which we may expect prayers when we are no more. Praises I should call it for fear of being thought Popish.'

The Admiral was unlucky. After all his labours he was thrown from his horse and died in 1723. His house and estate passed to his nephew, Captain Francis Blake Delaval, who completed the house by 1729 and the wings by 1755. The main house was completed under the capable direction of William Etty. Captain Francis had also inherited Ford Castle, Northumberland, from his mother's family.

The Delavals were a lively lot. Captain Francis had a large family, five daughters and eight sons, the best known of which was Sir

The impressive stables at Seaton Delaval Hall were fitted out later in the eighteenth century.

Francis Delaval, friend of Garrick and enthusiastic dramatist. Their family history is given in Francis Askham's *The Gay Delavals* (1955), which describes the entertainments laid on by the Delavals later in the eighteenth century, including rope dancers, 'a Pantomin entertainment' and 'Tilts, Tournements, Gamblings and Bull-batings.'

To accommodate a larger family, and these memorable romps, Seaton Delaval was extended in the later eighteenth century, but suffered a major fire in the early nineteenth century. The main block, including the tantalising double-height hall, was first re-roofed by John Dobson of Newcastle in the 1820s; only the wings have ever been re-inhabited since.

Seaton Delaval bears close comparison to Vanbrugh's last recorded major country house commission, Grimsthorpe Castle, unfinished at his death in 1726, and the last to be begun in 1723. Only one range of Vanbrugh's design was ever completed, but what a front it is. There can be no doubt that as you approach Grimsthorpe Castle by road even today, the building has the dignified presence of an ancient castle, dominating the wide open countryside in all directions, as much for Vanbrugh's crisp balustraded towers as for the older gabled ranges.

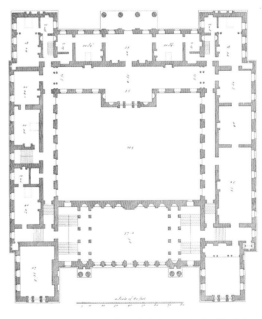

The overall outline was compared by Laurence Whistler in 1954 to the profile of Lumley Castle, as an echo of a fourteenth-century castle with emphatic corner towers. A complete transformation and refacing of the house was planned and a series of designs was published in the third volume of *Vitruvius Britannicus* (1725).

Above: The proposed, but unexecuted, plan for remodelling the full extent of Grimsthorpe Castle as it appeared in Vitruvius Britannicus, Vol III, 1725. *Only the north range was completed before Vanbrugh's death in 1726.*

Left: Ducal splendour: the muscular north entrance of Grimsthorpe Castle in Lincolnshire. This range was entirely remodelled by Vanbrugh from 1723; photographed in 2006.

The original house dated back to the fifteenth century and had been much rebuilt in the sixteenth century. It was the seat of Charles Brandon, Duke of Suffolk, who was married to Mary, Dowager Queen of France and sister of Henry VIII. After her death, the Duke married his ward, the heiress of the Lord Willoughby of Grimsthorpe.

It is said that the house was rebuilt before the visit of Henry VIII in 1541. The contemporary historian John Leland recorded: 'The Place of Grimsthorpe was no great thing afore the new building of the seconde court, yet was all the old work of Stone: the Gatehouse was faire and strong, and the waulles of either side of it embatelid.'

Vanbrugh's elevation replaced a late-seventeenth-century remodelling, and the balustrade is crowned in entirely Baroque spirit, with

Above and left: The drama of the main hall at Grimsthorpe Castle, Lincolnshire, is enhanced by the two-storied screens of arches, which are described in a late eighteenth-century inventory as music galleries. The hall is on a vast scale and the arcading runs around all four walls in different versions, with arched windows to the north. A blind arcade to the south is filled with paintings of English monarchs by Thornhill.

Overleaf: The concentration of windows on the north entrance wall of the hall makes the interior surprisingly light; the room has the feeling of a palace courtyard in Rome.

two sculptural groups, *Pluto and Proserpina*, after Bernini, and *Neptune and Amphitrite*, on either side of the Bertie arms. The whole is curiously Herculean, massive in the spirit perhaps of a Roman fort, but enlivened with the Earth and Water deities celebrating their loving triumphs, presumably a reference to the fertility of the land which this building dominates so effectively.

The seven-bay centrepiece of the entrance elevation, has, as Hussey and Tipping observed in 1927, 'the massiveness of a Roman amphitheatre' with two tiers of arched windows. It is framed between two solid-seeming pairs of banded Doric columns and the whole is in turn framed between two projecting walls leading to two-storey pavilions – miniature versions of the Italianate towers, at the west and east.

On the *piano nobile*, each of the main towers have the familiar motif of the Serliana windows: one marking the two-storey chapel (an existing room created in the 1670s), the other marking the State Dining Room. The towers are crowned by corner details in the manner of Roman veiled Bacchic altars that at a distance have the character of turrets. Both the forecourt pavilions and the west and east towers of the north range have the exaggerated keystone on the

ground floor, ultimately derived from Serlio; it is a motif much associated with Hawksmoor, but clearly used often by Vanbrugh too.

The initial patron at Grimsthorpe, Robert Bertie, was another kinsman with whom he had spent part of his youth when attached to the household of James Bertie, Earl of Abingdon, in the 1680s. Vanbrugh referred to Robert in a letter as 'my old Friend and Ally The Great Chamberlain'.

Robert Bertie had served under his uncle, Thomas Osborne (later 1st Duke of Leeds) who, as the Earl of Danby, had led a northern rising in support of William and Mary and been rewarded with the Chancellorship of the Duchy of Lancaster. Bishop Burnet described him as 'a fine gentleman, has both wit and learning', though Swift said, 'I never observed a grain of either'.

In 1704, Mackay described him as 'handsome in his person; of a fair complexion, has both wit and learning'. He inherited the hereditary position of Lord Great Chamberlain from his father in 1701.

Left: *Grimsthorpe Castle, Lincolnshire. The screen of arches at either end of the hall, lead to the staircases ascending to the first floor. The detailing of the door-cases is derived from the Capitoline Palace in Rome.*

Below: *The vaulted approach to the chapel.*

His wonderful monument by Henry Cheere and Scheemakers in the local parish church, St Michael's Edenham, shows him standing in full Roman dress.

The preliminary design for the north elevation, now in the Victoria and Albert Museum, is thought to have been done at the same time as Vanbrugh's dated survey in 1715, when Robert Bertie, 4th Earl of Lindsey, was made 1st Duke of Ancaster and Kesteven and had served as temporary Lord Justice following the accession of George I. Work did not begin until just after he had died in 1723.

This 1715 design for the north elevation is similar in overall effect to the finished elevation, although plainer without the more Italianate detail. It has the two-storey, round-arched arcade at the centre of the elevation. The addition of the detail by 1723 (the date on the engravings published in *Vitruvius Britannicus*, Vol III, 1725) seems to show Vanbrugh responding to the Palladian tastes of the day. The proposed south front with its central Corinthian portico seems particularly Palladian in spirit and to have little to do with the original design for the north front.

On 20 August 1723, Vanbrugh referred to a visit to the 2nd Duke at Grimsthorpe: 'to consult about his Building; by which I belive he is inclin'd to go upon the General Design I made for his Father last

Winter and which was approv'd of by himself.' It is thought that Vanbrugh may well have worked earlier for the Bertie family elsewhere on their estates, as designs amongst their papers and payments made before 1712 suggest. They are detailed in an article by John Lord in *Architectural History* (1991). Mr Lord also observed that the walls and pavilions of the forecourt do not appear in the *Vitruvius Britannicus* engravings, and may have been added later. They were completed by 1729–30, and are mentioned in the letters of a local mason, Edward Nutt.

John Harris noted in *Architectural Review* (1961) that these payments may refer to a house at Swinstead, the original Swinstead Hall, across the park, which was demolished in the nineteenth century, although some evidence of masonry and cellars can be identified. The 1725 inventory for that house, published in the 1907 Commission on Historic Monuments Report, mentioned a picture of Sir John Vanbrugh's Castle at Greenwich hanging there. Only the summer house survives, a curiously castellar structure with echoes of a triumphal arch, which is said to have been visible from both houses across the park, and was originally open on the ground floor.

It comes as a surprise to find that the whole of the north range between the two towers, all of which Vanbrugh altered, was previously one vast Tudor great hall, and still referred to as the Great Hall in eighteenth- and early-nineteenth-century inventories. The whole is a masterful creation, with the character of an elegant open arcaded court of distinctly Italianate flavour (with echoes perhaps of an open courtyard at the centre of an Italian palazzo). The ceiling, floor and arcades are clearly all designed of a piece, the pattern of the large oval compartment reflected in the pattern of the floor.

Inside the Great Hall, at each end, Vanbrugh inserted two open arcades on two levels with ironwork staircases leading up to dramatic doorways on the first floor. These arcades have a curious double-skinned architectural effect, being both thick in appearance and thin in character, because this ingenious arcading is formed by two tiers of five arches with a narrow space in between, providing a platform which could potentially accommodate musicians or other performers. They are referred to in the 1780 inventory as music galleries.

The doorways at the top of these stairs were identified by the scholar, Rudolf Wittkower, as based on Michelangelo's doors for the

Right: *The Serliana window of the chapel at Grimsthorpe Castle, Lincolnshire was inserted by Vanbrugh. The chapel's interior dates mostly from the 1680s.*

Below: *The vaulted hall refaced in stone by Vanbrugh.*

side palaces of the Capitol in Rome, known in England from the engravings by Specchi, which were published in 1702 in Domenico de Rossi's *Studio d'architettura civile*. It has been suggested that this might be part of the finishing-off idea to have been carried out by Hawksmoor – a drawing for the Duke of Ancaster's chapel was mentioned in the sale of Hawksmoor's effects after his death.

Vanbrugh's intention, as can be seen from the *Vitruvius Britannicus* plan, was to move the state rooms to the west front, with a great saloon on the south front behind the proposed portico, but the work was discontinued, either because another generation did not wish to spend the money or the idea simply ran out of steam after the death of Vanbrugh himself in 1726. The building was brought to an end after the completion of the north front and only part of the west wing. The rest of the west wing was remodelled in a Neo-Tudor style in 1811; the south remains a curious, if attractive hotch-potch of periods.

The proposed plan shows a gallery that would have run around the three sides of the courtyard. Other spaces remodelled by Vanbrugh

include the vaulted hall to the east. He introduced the Serliana or Venetian windows to the present State Dining Room on the west corner and to the late-seventeenth-century chapel on the east, but his remodelling got no further, or at least no further evidence survives.

One of the most extraordinary features of the arcaded Great Hall, is the series of seven English kings painted in the 1720s by Sir James Thornhill: William I, Edward III, Henry V, George I, William III, Henry VIII, and Henry VII. The early kings are similar in subject and form to the late sixteenth-century full-length paintings that hung at Lumley Castle when Vanbrugh worked there (and can now be seen at Leeds Castle in Kent). They therefore may be monarchs associated with national liberties and martial prowess, rather than just those associated with the Willoughby family.

The grandeur of this sequence of royal portraits, probably suggested by the historically conscious Vanbrugh, also underlines the public quality of this extraordinary space. Entered through a massive fort-like entrance, it is surprisingly light, and the screens of arches add to the theatre of the space. The hall is heavy with Classical and historical allusion, speaks of Vanbrugh's forceful and original imagination.

Above: *The east front of Grimsthorpe Castle, Lincolnshire, in 1924. Vanbrugh's tower is to the right.*

Left: *A glimpse through a side gate of the north front.*

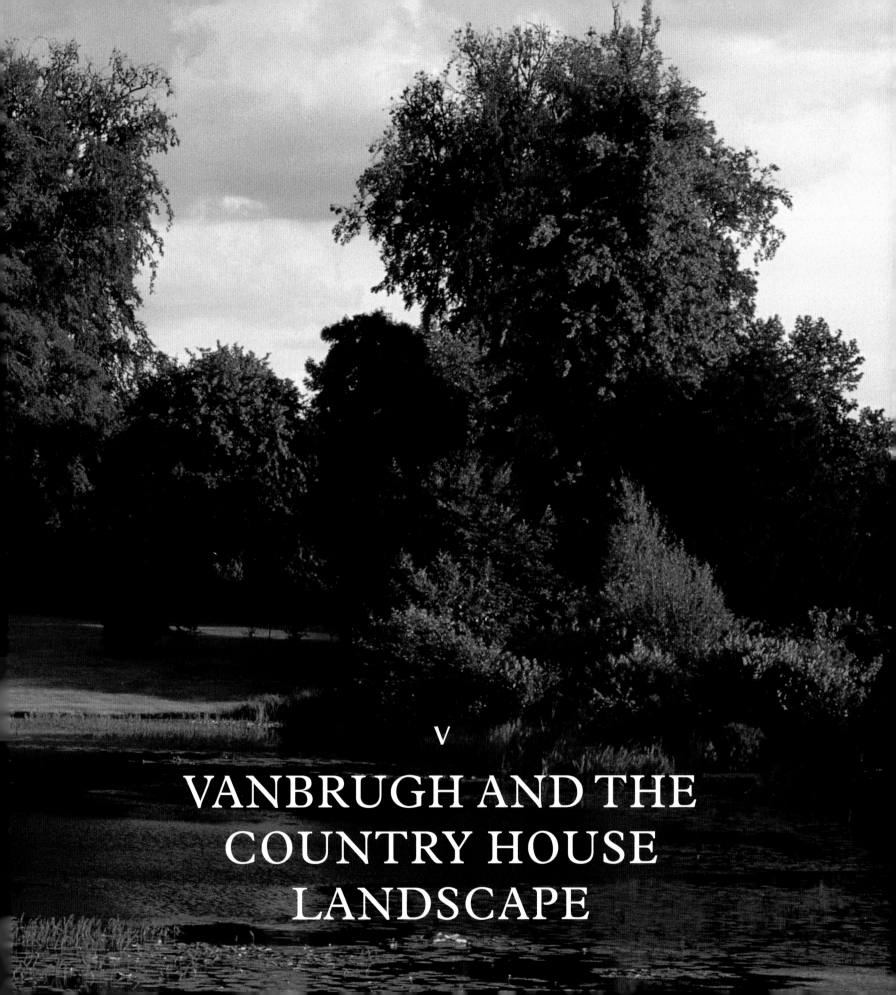

V

VANBRUGH AND THE COUNTRY HOUSE LANDSCAPE

It is easy to be so dazzled by Vanbrugh's great houses that we can overlook his considerable contribution to some of the greatest landscape gardens in England. He played a role, not only at Castle Howard and Blenheim, but also at Stowe where he advised and collaborated with Sir Richard Temple (later 1st Viscount Cobham) for some twenty years. At Stowe, he designed numerous buildings, some of which survive, although others were later taken down as the gardens continued to expand. Indeed, most of the landscapes in which Vanbrugh was involved have changed out of recognition. However, Castle Howard, perhaps, more than any other still evokes the Vanbrugh-inspired landscape, recalling the flavour of Antiquity and the Roman Campagna in particular.

Vanbrugh never professed to be a landscape designer but he always worked alongside professionals, including George London, Henry Wise, Stephen Switzer and Charles Bridgeman. Perhaps the well-travelled imaginative Vanbrugh broke the bounds in this territory through his conversations with the great gardeners, resolving with them how his houses, temples, bridges, walls and terraces would work with their grand formal planted schemes and canals.

It was, perhaps, his vision of the totality of things, and his over-arching sense of drama that defined his collaborative work with landscape designers. His idea of the relationship of terrain and temple, scale and setting is exemplified most effectively in the dramatic bridge at Blenheim, in which he contrived several rooms, perhaps as banqueting houses, and intended to place a grotto.

His sense of history and poetry were key certainly, but there was, too, something of the soldier's eye for mapping a terrain and identifying its utility. And there was also an underlying ideal of the Classical world; a world he knew from his own education and reading, as well as from conversations with other writers, patrons and his well-read assistant, Nicholas Hawksmoor.

The summary of the Classical authors on gardens and landscape given in the introduction to his collaborator Stephen Switzer's

Previous pages: *A Classical arcadia: one of the Doric lake pavilions designed by Vanbrugh for Lord Cobham at Stowe, Buckinghamshire.*

Above: *Blenheim Palace, Oxfordshire, designed by Vanbrugh and begun in 1705, seen here from the north-east. His famous Grand Bridge, with its 100-foot main arch, is thought to be the finest in Europe. The lake was enlarged by Capability Brown in the 1760s.*

Ichnographia Rustica (1718) lists some of the familiar sources: Cato, Varro, Columella, Palladius and Pliny. It has been suggested, for instance, that the gardens at Eastbury, as engraved in *Vitruvius Britannicus*, Vol III, 1725, were modelled on the famous approach to the Ancient Roman Temple of Fortune at Praeneste (Palestrina), which sat on rising terraces.

Although Vanbrugh appears not to have travelled to Rome to see the great antiquities at first-hand, an idea of the ancient world may well have been fostered in his fertile imagination from an early age by his father, Giles, who had spent a year in Rome for his education.

Vanbrugh's interest in landscape, his visual imagination and sense of the scenographic qualities of buildings are surely evident in all his architecture: in the outlines and the sense of place. It was this quality of his work which Sir Joshua Reynolds later called 'the conduct of the background', in his *Discourse XIII*, based on his Royal Academy lectures in 1786.

Vanbrugh's role as a precursor to the Picturesque has been much debated. It is interesting to note that Richard Payne Knight in his famous *An Analytical Inquiry into the Principles of Taste* (1805) wrote on the proper siting of a country house, arguing that 'more consideration ought to be had of the view towards it, than those of fromwards it'.

He continued: 'Sir John Vanbrugh is the only architect, I know of, who has either planned or placed his houses according to the principle here recommended; and, in his two chief works, Blenheim and Castle Howard, it appears to have been strictly adhered to, at least in the placing of them.' He went on, after some unflattering remarks about the views from the principal fronts, 'but the situations of both as objects to the surrounding scenery, are the best that could have been chosen.'

If this was the secret of the success of the siting of his buildings, it should also be noted that Vanbrugh, as architect, was the master of the smaller temple and belvedere, and, as Giles Worsley noted, he was often more scrupulously Classical or Palladian in these than in his house design. Examples of this include his Doric lake pavilions at Stowe, the lost Bagnio and the lost temple at Eastbury (a vast structure, engraved for *Vitruvius Britannicus*, with a Corinthian Order

portico that was as high as that of the Pantheon), and the delicate surviving garden temples at Kings Weston, near Bristol.

But this is not to say that Vanbrugh's ingenious castle style was not expressed in the design of garden buildings. One of the most memorable surviving examples of his 'embattled manner' on the smaller scale is a simple, castellated brick-built belvedere at Claremont of about 1715–20, belonging to a landscaped garden which once served Vanbrugh's own home there, then known as Chargate.

He sold the house to (and extended it for) his patron, Thomas Pelham-Holles, the Earl of Clare (later 1st Duke of Newcastle), collaborating from then on with Charles Bridgeman as the landscape designer. Bridgeman succeeded Henry Wise as Royal Gardener to George II and Queen Caroline.

Whether this belvedere should be seen as medieval in inspiration or Roman is an interesting question – perhaps the two were deliberately combined. Most of the gardens and landscapes of Vanbrugh's houses feature mock-fortified walls and bastions (at Castle Howard over half a mile's worth), which at Blenheim, around the wilderness, Stephen Switzer described in 1718 as, 'after the ancient Roman manner.'

Colen Campbell's description of the belvedere at Claremont in *Vitruvius Britannicus*, Vol III, 1725) captured the Arcadian quality of the landscape: 'The Situation … [is] singularly romantick, and from the high Tower has a most prodigious fine Prospect of the Thames and adjacent villas.' This echoes Pliny's famous letters describing his country retreats, Villa Laurentium and Villa Tusculum. That on Laurentium described the pleasures of a comfortable retreat set in its own gardens, with views of water and neighbouring villas.

The magnificent contrived landscape at Castle Howard was developed over some forty years with several key contributions from both Hawksmoor and Vanbrugh. It required the removal of the old village and church of Henderskelfe. The sequence of the designs seems to be: the walled garden, with the famous Satyr Gate of 1705, the 1714 obelisk raised to honour the victories of Marlborough, and the Pyramid Gate, dated 1719, all designed by Vanbrugh, as was the

Above: *Compact and precise: the lake pavilions at Stowe seen obliquely.*

Right: *The Rotondo at Stowe, Buckinghamshire, designed by Vanbrugh, although the profile of the dome was altered later in the eighteenth century.*

belvedere, now known as the Temple of the Four Winds, designed by 1724 and completed after his death.

It appears likely that the pyramid erected as a monument to Lord William Howard, founder of Lord Carlisle's particular dynasty, designed by Hawksmoor and built by 1728, would have been discussed with Vanbrugh. It is interesting to reflect on the proximity

Top (left): *The bastioned wall which encloses the immediate parkland of Castle Howard, Yorkshire.*
(right): *The Carrmire Gate at Castle Howard, designed by Hawksmoor, continuing the theme of Vanbrugh's bastions, and built in the late 1720s.*

Above: *The belvedere at Claremont, near Esher, Surrey, with its admired views looking down to the River Thames.*

Left: *Power in simplicity: the boldly tapered garden walls at Claremont, Surrey.*

of the crenellated walls, which suggest a direct allusion to the Pyramid of Caius Cestius and the Porta San Paolo in Rome. Hawksmoor's freestanding mausoleum to Lord Carlisle is also very much in sympathy with Vanbrugh's vision.

At Castle Howard, George London drew up plans in around 1700 for Wray Wood, the existing area of woodland near the then proposed new house, but Carlisle decided to reject that plan. Switzer wrote admiringly in *Ichnographia Rustica* (1718) of 'that beautiful wood belonging to the Earl of Carlisle, at Castle Howard, where Mr London designed a Star, which would have spoiled the wood; but that thus his Lordship's superlative Genius prevented it, and to the great Advancement of the design, has given it that Labyrinth diverting Model we now see it.' The military-style bastion walls which encased Wray Wood at Castle Howard may have been innovations of Vanbrugh and Carlisle together.

Vanbrugh's sophisticated awareness of how buildings work in a landscape, of the way they stimulate the imagination with historical and aesthetic associations, found clearest expression in a letter he wrote on 9 June 1709. In this, he tried to persuade the Duchess of Marlborough to retain the remains of the old royal manor of Woodstock, which he sought to keep within sight of the new house. It is worth quoting at some length, as an early expression of preservation philosophy.

He argued: 'There is perhaps no one thing, which the most Polite part of Mankind have more universally agreed in than the Vallue they have ever set upon the Remains of distant Times Nor amongst the Severall kinds of those Antiquitys, are there any so much regarded, as those of Buildings; Some for their Magnificence, or Curious Workmanship; And others; as they move more lively and pleasing Reflections (than History without their Aid can do) On the Persons who have Inhabited them; On the Remarkable things which have been transacted in them, Or the extraordinary Occasions of Erecting them.'

'As I believe it cannot be doubted, but if Travellers many Ages hence, shall be shewn The Very House in which so great a Man Dwelt, as they will then read the Duke of Marlborough in Story;

And that they Shall be told, it was only his Favourite Habitation, but was Erected for him by the Bounty of the Queen And with the Approbation of the People, As a Monument of the Greatest Services and Honours, that any subject had ever done his Country: I believe, tho' they may not find Art enough in the Builder, to make them Admire the Beauty of the Fabrick they will find Wonder enough in the Story to make em pleas'd with the Sight of it.'

He applied the same argument to the old manor, 'rais'd by One of the Bravest and most Warlike of the English kings' (Henry II), imagining those who will go 'to See what Ancient Remains are to be found of Rosamond's Bower' (the retreat of Henry's lover). Furthermore, in his words: 'if the Historicall Argument Stands in need of Assistance; there is Still much to be said on Other Considerations.'

He added: 'That Part of the Park which is Seen from the North Front of the New Building, has little Variety of Objects Nor dos the Country beyond it Afford any of Vallue, It therefore Stands in Need of all the helps that can be given, which are only Five; Buildings, And Plantations. These rightly dispos'd will indeed Supply all wants of Nature in that Place. And the Most Agreeable Disposition is to Mix them.'

Namely, he argued in favour of planting a thicket, 'So that all the Building left (which is only the Habitable Part and the Chappel) might Appear in Two Risings amongst 'em, it wou'd make One of the Most Agreeable Objects that the best Landskip Painters can invent.' It could be described as one of the first recorded expressions of the Picturesque principle and one of the most eloquent. By the 'best Landksip painters' he would have meant Claude and Poussin, with their distinctive fictive architecture.

His recommendation was turned down by the suspicious Duchess. She discovered that he had repaired rooms in the manor to use as his residence while he visited the site, and she ordered it to be destroyed. In 1719, Vanbrugh wrote in defence of retaining what was called the Holbein Gateway at Whitehall on associational grounds – again unsuccessfully.

From 1719, until his death, Vanbrugh also contributed temples, and, no doubt, ideas and encouragement, to the landscape around the main mansion at Stowe. He is thought to have added the great temple front portico on the north entrance front of the 1680s house. The park there (now preserved by the National Trust) was created by his friend, the 4th Baronet, Sir Richard Temple, who in 1714 became the 1st Baron Cobham and 1st Viscount in 1718. Work had begun in 1714 along formal lines.

Lord Cobham was a fellow member of the Kit-Cat Club and a leading Whig. He was another of Vanbrugh's man-of-action patrons, a distinguished soldier who had served with Marlborough and famously led the assault on Vigo in Spain. He had also recently married Anne Halsey, the daughter of a wealthy Southwark brewer.

Roman drama: the Pyramid, designed by Hawksmoor in 1728, stands close to a castle-like bastion by Vanbrugh at Castle Howard, Yorkshire.

Above: *The Temple of the Four Winds, Castle Howard, photographed in 2001.*

Left: *The portico of the Temple of the Four Winds, Castle Howard, Vanbrugh's last temple, looking back towards the main house; photographed in 1926.*

Here, as at Eastbury in Dorset, Vanbrugh worked alongside the designer Charles Bridgeman and his designs for several very different temples may have influenced Bridgeman in his arrangements of the gardens. George Vertue's notebooks, 1745, referred to their individual contributions thus: 'Sir John Vanbrugh who was most concerned in the direction of Lord Cobham's gardens or rather buildings because Mr. Bridgeman Gardiner to the King had the direction & disposition of the Gardens.' Between 1720 and 1724 they transformed the scale of the gardens.

They were much admired by contemporaries, but while some of the temples survive, the nature of the landscape has changed considerably since Vanbrugh's day. Lord Perceval wrote of Stowe in 1724 that the beauty of this garden is that it is 'not bounded by walls, but by a ha ha which leaves you the sight of a bewtiful wooded country ... a great number of walk, terminated by summer houses & heathen temples of different structures and adorned with statues cast from the Anticks'. He also observed: 'we all know how chargeable it is to Make a garden with tast: to make one of a sudden is more so ... I doubt not but much of his wife's great fortune has been sunk in it.'

The temples, which are known to have been designed by Vanbrugh (all can seen on a bird's eye view drawn up by Bridgeman in 1720), include: the pair of open-fronted Doric lake pavilions, which framed the avenue on axis with the house and once served as entrance lodges for visitors to the gardens; the Guglio, an obelisk which stood in an octagonal pool, intended to spout water; and the Temple of Sleep, or the Sleeping Parlour, a simpler version of Vanbrugh's belevedere at Castle Howard, and the Temple of the Four Winds, which was taken down during further expansions of the garden later in the eighteenth century.

At the centre of the new and longer walks and vistas created by Bridgeman stood the Rotondo. This does survive, although the domed roof was altered by the architect Borra at the request of the 1st Earl Temple. But at first, the temple was the focus of the gardens, as extended by Bridgeman and Vanbrugh, and the views to and from this temple were critical.

Vanbrugh also contributed a number of monuments which are completely lost: the King's Pillar, which carried a statue of the Prince of Wales, later George II, possibly by Rysbrack, and the Queen's Pillar, a group of four Ionic columns supporting a statue of the Princess of Wales, later Queen Caroline, also thought to have been by Rysbrack.

Vanbrugh designed Nelson's Seat, named after a Stowe gardener (a custom adopted by Lord Cobham after the example of Pliny the Younger), and an unusual brick temple (later stuccoed and renamed the Temple of Bacchus), Coucher's Obelisk, a monument to the Reverend Coucher, chaplain to the regiment commanded by Temple. He also designed Dido's cave, painted with the loves of Aeneas and Dido, described in 1732 as a 'private grotto'.

Vanbrugh's last design for Stowe was a steep pyramid, some 60ft high (illustrated by George Bickham in *The Beauties of Stow* in 1750), again presumably inspired by the pyramid of Caius Cestius. After Vanbrugh's death, Cobham inscribed the pyramid as a memorial to him – a tribute to his friend who had helped shape his house and his gardens.

Vanbrugh must have revelled in the opportunity to make real the Temple's quirky family motto, '*Templa quam dilecta*' (how beautiful are thy temples), a phrase from *The Book of Psalms* (Psalm 84). Certainly Vanbrugh delighted in the whole achievement at Stowe, in which he felt closely involved and which brought him personal pleasure.

In 1719, he visited Stowe and found Cobham 'very well, and in very good humour: and much entertain'd with (beside his Wife) the improvements of his House and Gardens, in which he Spends all he has to Spare.' On 12 August 1725, Vanbrugh wrote to his friend, Tonson, of a tour he was taking partly in the company of Lord Carlisle: 'The Company were so well pleas'd at Stowe, that they stay'd four days, My Lord Carlisle then went on for Castle Howard, and we Stay'd at Stowe a Fortnight, a Place now, so Agreeable, that I had much ado to leave it at all.'

This was a year before he died and it is pleasing, in a scene so different from his last reception at Blenheim, to think of him drinking in his achievements, enjoying the hospitality of the paradise he had helped to create, a respected friend and confidant of the cultivated and active patron, Viscount Cobham, for whom he had developed outward-looking houses, with evocative vistas and elegant temples drawing the eye.

Above: *Vanbrugh's Pyramid Gateway at Castle Howard, Yorkshire, looking towards the 1714 obelisk erected to celebrate Marlborough's victories.*

Right: *A detail of the Satyr Gateway at Castle Howard, designed by Vanbrugh and Hawksmoor in 1705, and carved by Samuel Carpenter.*

VI

VANBRUGH TODAY

Vanbrugh's great country houses remain icons of early-eighteenth-century architecture: ambitions and dreams, expressed with extraordinary vitality and vivacity, in practical and surprisingly manageable plan forms (remember how Adam praised Vanbrugh's knowledge of 'the art of living among the great').

Vanbrugh's reputation has endured. His work remained a subject of fascination for many in the twentieth century. It even, surprisingly, had a place in English Brutalism in the 1960s, which drew on the more elemental qualities of Vanbrugh's style. In the late 1940s, Peter Smithson, who studied architecture at Newcastle, and later England's leading Brutalist, made a measured survey of Vanbrugh's Seaton Delaval Hall. In the next decade, Quinlan Terry, the architect of so many modern Classical country houses, was also inspired to make a survey of Seaton Delaval Hall, while a student at the Architectural Association. With two other students, he camped out in the blackened shell of the main range of the house.

The continuing stories of Vanbrugh's houses, which inevitably were re-decorated, re-fitted and furnished in the later eighteenth and nineteenth centuries, remain as compelling as the story of their creations. The astonishing revival of Castle Howard – begun after a devastating fire in 1940 which burnt out the dome and twenty other rooms, while the house was home to an evacuated girls' school – is an inspiring story.

The process of restoration at Castle Howard was begun by George

Howard, later Lord Howard of Henderskelfe, who took over in 1946, and continues today under his son, the Hon. Simon Howard, who lives there with his wife Rebecca and their two children. The house was first opened to the public in 1952, although the memorable skyline was without its dome until it was rebuilt in 1960–61.

When, in 1978, the house was used as a setting for the television drama version of *Brideshead Revisited*, the garden hall, on the south side of the main hall, was restored and the walls painted by Felix Kelly with a series of murals depicting fantastic buildings and landscape inspired by Vanbrugh's style and mood. The television series had a major impact on the public's imagination and played its part in transforming the reputation of country houses in general. In 2008, a new film version of Waugh's novel, again filmed at Castle Howard, has brought the spirit of Vanbrugh's architecture to a new public.

Above: Grimsthorpe Castle is today preserved by a trust and remains the seat of Lady Willoughby de Eresby, descendant of the original patron.

Left: Like a castle from a painting by Claude: Blenheim Palace seen from the west. It is still the home of the Duke of Marlborough and one of Britain's best known country houses.

Blenheim Palace, additionally famous in the twentieth century as the birthplace of one of Marlborough's most famous descendants, Sir Winston Churchill, remains the proud home of the 11th Duke of Marlborough and is much visited by an international public, lying as it does, close to Oxford and the gateway to the Cotswolds beyond. It is beautifully maintained and preserved, the subject of a continuing process of restoration – only last year the six statues of Roman allegorical figures on the north front were copied and replaced, reviving a note of Baroque swagger.

Grimsthorpe Castle, with its palatial north front by Vanbrugh, is owned by a trust, and remains the seat of Lady Willoughby de Eresby, a descendant of the original patron of Vanbrugh, and like Castle Howard and Blenheim preserved in magnificent condition as one of the great treasure houses of England.

Seaton Delaval Hall was until recently the much-loved family home of Lord Hastings, who died in 2007, a descendant of the Delaval patron. The late Lord Hastings re-roofed the main range and then restored the kitchen wing, which became his residence in 1990. It is currently the subject of a campaign to be it acquired by the National

Trust. Lumley Castle remained a seat of the earls of Scarborough until the late twentieth century and has been a hotel since 1976.

Kimbolton Castle was sold in 1950 by the 10th Duke of Manchester to become a boarding school. While Kings Weston, surrounded by urban development and threatened with demolition in 1955, was for many years in use as a police college. After standing empty for some time, it is now a wedding venue owned and run by Mr John Hardy. Eastbury and Vanbrugh Castle are private homes, while the belvedere at Claremont and the surviving three temples at Stowe are now in the care of the National Trust and tactfully restored. The main house at Stowe became a school in the 1920s.

The critic Jonathan Meades has recently noted the visits said to be made by the French Neo-Classical architect Ledoux: 'Just looking at Ledoux's work is bound to prompt the idea he knew Vanbrugh's. There is an unquestionable visual, sculptural connection between the two which causes one to question the pigeon-holing of Vanbrugh as "baroque". In his later and more *outré* work he obviously wasn't. He was *sui generis* or at least a neo-Classicist *avant la lettre*. He's an illustration of Jean Francois Revel's dictum that "there are no styles only talents". He excites an emotional response which has nothing to do with style.'

Architect Sir Richard MacCormac, who has been inspired by the work of Vanbrugh in his new buildings for St John's College, Oxford, and Trinity College, Cambridge, (Burrell's Field) also comments: 'Vanbrugh and Hawksmoor had a maverick interpretation of the Classical that Burlington and his school stamped on. Vanbrugh's buildings, like Michelangelo's Capitoline Palace, have a presence that can out-stare the viewer – you are being challenged by the very scale of the building. I also feel that Vanbrugh thought historically, and that his architecture always had a narrative.'

Vanbrugh's country houses rank amongst the most memorable in England, so it is not surprising that they have been so well represented in *Country Life* magazine. This book is a homage to the extraordinary story of Vanbrugh, the man and the artist, who transformed ambitions and dreams into an enduring reality.

Above: *The continuing life of a Vanbrugh house: Kimbolton Castle is now a private school, while Lumley Castle is a hotel and Kings Weston a wedding venue.*

Right: *The Rotondo at Stowe, Buckinghamshire. The landscaped gardens are now in the care of the National Trust, who have restored many of the temples, and replaced a gilded figure of Venus seen here.*

SELECT BIBLIOGRAPHY

INTRODUCTION & GENERAL

Beard, Geoffrey, *The Work of John Vanbrugh*, B. T. Batsford, 1986.

Blunt, Anthony (ed.), *Baroque and Rococo: Architecture and Decoration*, Elek, 1978.

Colvin, Howard, entries on 'Vanbrugh' and 'Hawksmoor' in *Biographical Dictionary of British Architects 1600–1840*, Yale University Press, 1995.

—, Colvin, Howard and Craig, Maurice (eds.) *Architectural Drawing in the Library of Elton Hall: Vanbrugh and Pearce*, Roxburghe Club, 1964.

Dobrée, Bonamy (ed.), *The Complete Works of Sir John Vanbrugh: Vol I–III, The Plays*, Nonesuch Press, 1928.

Downes, Kerry, *English Baroque Architecture*, A. Zwemmer, 1966.

—, *Vanbrugh*, A. Zwemmer, 1977.

—, *Sir John Vanbrugh: A Biography*, St Martin's Press, 1987.

Girouard, Mark, *Life in the English Country House*, Yale University Press, 1987.

Hart, Vaughan, 'Vanbrugh's Travels' in *History Today*, July 1992, pp.26–32.

—, *Nicholas Hawksmoor: Rebuilding Ancient Wonders*, Yale University Press, 2002.

—, *Sir John Vanbrugh: Storyteller in Stone*, Yale University Press, 2008.

Hoppit, Julian, *A Land of Liberty? England 1689–1727*, Oxford University Press, 2000.

Lees-Milne, James, *English Country Houses: Baroque, 1685–1715*, Country Life, 1970.

McCormick, Frank, *Sir John Vanbrugh: the Playwright as Architect*, Penn State University Press, 1991.

—, *Sir John Vanbrugh: A Reference Guide*, G. K. Hall, 1992.

Montgomery-Massingberd, Hugh, *Great Houses of England and Wales*, Laurence King, 1994.

New Oxford Dictionary of National Biography (2004–08) Oxford University Press.

Ridgway, Christopher and Williams, Robert, (eds.), *Sir John Vanbrugh and Landscape Architecture in Baroque England 1690–1730*, Alan Sutton/National Trust, 2000.

Summerson, John, *Architecture in Britain 1530–1830*, Penguin, 1955.

Tipping, H. Avray and Hussey, Christopher, *In English Homes: Period IV: Vol II: The Works of John Vanbrugh and His School 1699–1736*, Country Life, 1928.

Turner, Jane, (ed.), *The Dictionary of Art*, Macmillan and Groves Dictionary, 1996, revd 1998.

Webb, Geoffrey (ed.), *The Complete Works of Sir John Vanbrugh: Vol IV, The Letters*, Nonesuch Press, 1928.

Whistler, Laurence, *The Imagination of Vanbrugh and His Fellow Artists*, B. T. Batsford, 1954.

Worsley, Giles, *Classical Architecture in Britain the Heroic Age*, Yale University Press, 1995.

CASTLE HOWARD

Downes, Kerry, *Vanbrugh*, A. Zwemmer, 1977.

Ridgway, Christopher, '1699–1999, A Dome for All Seasons', *Country Life*, April 1, 1999.

—, *Castle Howard Guidebook*, 1997, revised 2005.

Saumarez Smith, Charles, *The Building of Castle Howard*, Pimlico, 1990.

BLENHEIM PALACE

Blenheim Palace Guidebook.

Downes, Kerry, *Vanbrugh*, A. Zwemmer, 1977.

Green, David, *Blenheim Palace, Oxfordshire*, Country Life, 1952.

Worsley, Giles, 'Sir John Vanbrugh and the Search for a National Style', *Gothic Architecture and its Meaning 1550–1830*, pp.99–134, ed. Michael Hall, Spire Books, 2000.

ENCHANTED CASTLES

Downes, Kerry, 'The little colony on Greenwich Hill: Vanbrugh's field at Blackheath', *Country Life*, May 27, 1976.

Thurley, Simon, 'Kimbolton Castle', *Country Life*, March 30, 2006.

VANBRUGH'S LAST GREAT HOUSES

Askham, Francis, *The Gay Delavals*, Jonathan Cape, 1955.

Jackson-Stops, Gervase, 'Grimsthorpe Castle, Lincolnshire, I and II', *Country Life*, Nov 26 and Dec 3, 1987.

Hart, Vaughan, 'A Pretty Impudent Countenance: John Vanbrugh's Seaton Delaval', *Architectural Research Quarterly*, pp.7, 313–323, 2003.

Knox, Tim, *Grimsthorpe Guidebook*, 1996, revised 2003.

Lord, John, 'Sir John Vanbrugh and the Duke of Ancaster: Newly Discovered Documents', *Architectural History*, Vol 134, pp.136–144, 1991.

VANBRUGH AND THE COUNTRY HOUSE LANDSCAPE

Bevington, Michael, *Stowe House*, Paul Holberton, 2002.

Gibbon, Michael, 'Stowe Buckinghamshire: The House and Garden Buildings and Their Designers', *Architectural History*, Vol 20, pp.31–44, 82–83, 1977.

Mowl, Tim, *William Kent*, Jonathan Cape, 2006.

Richardson, Tim, *Arcadian Friends: Inventing the English Landscape Garden*, Bantam Press, 2007.

Robinson, John Martin, *Temples of Delight: Stowe Landscape Gardens*, George Philip/National Trust, 1990.

Watkin, David, *The English Vision: The Picturesque in Architecture, Landscape and Garden Design*, John Murray, 1982.

SUNDAY, 12TH. JUNE, 2011.

SUNDAY, 12TH. JUNE, 2011.